"Rachel Norment's *Dream Explorations . . .* is a gift to us all! The combination of her careful attention to her own dreams over decades, and her keen eye for the dreams and insights of other dreamers has produced a work of great depth, wisdom, and inspiration. It is a joy to read."

—**Jeremy Taylor**, D.Min., co-founder and past president of the International Association for the Study of Dreams, (IASD), founder-director of the Marin Institute for Projective Dream Work, (MIPD), and author of *The Wisdom of Your Dreams*

∾

"Rachel Norment is a seasoned traveler who knows how to navigate through her unconscious self. Serious dream workers and seekers after self-knowledge will be delighted by this book. Her practical insights, some new to me, into her personal symbols and themes are sure to bring light and guidance to anyone's inner explorations. I highly recommend it."

—**Jean Benedict Raffa**, Ph.D., author of *The Bridge to Wholeness, Dream Theatres of the Soul,* and *Healing the Sacred Divide*

∾

"*Dream Explorations* by Rachel Norment is a journey book, perfect for anyone ready to take that dive. . . into the deeper reaches of the inner self. There's a lot of dream books out now, all kinds. What distinguishes Rachel's creation from others is the skillful way she takes you by the hand and walks you through her life as if it were yours. You learn, because what she did also applies to you. And she doesn't miss a beat, tackling every possible subject, from toilets to sex to snakes to marriage to deaths to (the real biggie for all of us): finding our voice, our purpose in life—through the archetypal magic of dreams. A helpful and enjoyable book."

—**P. M. H. Atwater**, L.H.D., author of *Near-Death Experiences: The Rest of the Story, Future Memory,* and *Children of the Fifth World,* among others.

∾

"In this valuable and highly readable book, longtime dreamworker Rachel Norment offers us her collection of dream treasures with instructive reflections on common symbols and dream themes. This book clearly illustrates the rewards of a lifetime of dreamwork to guide and heal our lives."

—**Chelsea Wakefield**, Ph.D., LCSW., psychotherapist and author of *Negotiating the Inner Peace Treaty: Becoming The Person You Were Born To Be*

∾

"Because she has put her dreams to personal use in the healing process, with excellent results, Rachel Norment's understanding of dreams is knowledgeable and astute. *Dream Explorations* is a valuable read for all dreamers."

—**Jean Campbell,** past-president of the International Association for the Study of Dreams and author of *Group Dreaming: Dreams to the Tenth Power*

Chelsea,
I greatly appreciate your reading my manuscript and giving me such a gracious endorsement—
Best wishes, Rachel

Dream Explorations

A Journey in Self-Knowledge and Self-Realization

RACHEL G. NORMENT, M.A.

BALBOA.
PRESS
A DIVISION OF HAY HOUSE

Balboa Press books may be ordered through booksellers or by contacting:

Balboa Press
A Division of Hay House
1663 Liberty Drive
Bloomington, IN 47403
www.balboapress.com
1-(877) 407-4847

Because of the dynamic nature of the Internet, any web addresses or links contained in this book may have changed since publication and may no longer be valid. The views expressed in this work are solely those of the author and do not necessarily reflect the views of the publisher, and the publisher hereby disclaims any responsibility for them.

The author of this book does not dispense medical advice or prescribe the use of any technique as a form of treatment for physical, emotional, or medical problems without the advice of a physician, either directly or indirectly. The intent of the author is only to offer information of a general nature to help you in your quest for emotional and spiritual well-being. In the event you use any of the information in this book for yourself, which is your constitutional right, the author and the publisher assume no responsibility for your actions.

Any people depicted in stock imagery provided by Thinkstock are models, and such images are being used for illustrative purposes only.
Certain stock imagery © Thinkstock.

Printed in the United States of America.

ISBN: 978-1-4525-7753-1 (sc)
ISBN: 978-1-4525-7755-5 (hc)
ISBN: 978-1-4525-7754-8 (e)

Library of Congress Control Number: 2013912268

Balboa Press rev. date: 9/18/2013

To Owen,
my beloved husband,
whose supportive presence
in my life for more than 56 years
has contributed greatly
to my process of individuation.

CONTENTS

FOREWORD

When I first met Rachel Norment many years ago, I knew we were kindred spirits; since then we have become not only colleagues but also very close friends. Sharing dreams for many years, we have come to know each other in a very special way.

In 2005 I became co-creator of a Cancer Project sponsored by the International Association for the Study of Dreams (IASD). Our main goal was to develop teaching materials and to present dream work in cancer support communities across the country.

Rachel Norment was one of the first facilitators for the IASD Cancer Project, now called the IASD Health Care Project. Rachel's first book, published in 2006, has been an inspiration and model for many survivors. *Guided by Dreams: Breast Cancer, Dreams, and Transformation* is an amazing account of how she was guided and supported by her dreams as she went through diagnosis and treatment. All along the path to recovery, dreams were constant companions that brought Rachel insight, a sense of meaning and direction into healing, and a sense of purpose for the future.

Rachel's first book continues to be an invaluable resource for many people who must confront the challenge of cancer and for the IASD Health Care Project as we expand our outreach to others facing any kind of illness and trauma.

After the publication of *Guided by Dreams*, Rachel periodically told me about her desire to organize and share a collection of additional personal dreams dating from as early as the 1970's. I encouraged her, not realizing the enormity of her treasure trove of recorded dreams. I never imagined the time it would take to review her daunting stacks of dream journals or how much work and insight it would require to sort and arrange the selections.

Rachel has proved to be a first class, innovative curator. Reading her new book, *Dream Explorations: A Journey in Self-Knowledge and Self-Realization,* is like exploring an intriguing exhibit of fine art. From thousands of dreams, Rachel has carefully selected 245 and has arranged them according to themes and recurring imagery into an astonishing collection. The topics range from bathrooms and animals to healing encounters and experiences of spiritual seeking. With each topic and series of dreams, the readers can feel the impact of mysterious creative power and, through the author's thoughtful reflections on the multiple possibilities of meanings of each dream, can discover how to assimilate and integrate the energies and insights of their own dreams. Each dream series is a demonstration of how the psyche invites the dreamer to open up into larger life by responding to creative energies of the patterns of recurring dream imagery and themes.

Dream Explorations emphasizes the multi-dimensional nature of dream exploration. Dreams are pathways to health and wholeness, and every dream can bring multiple simultaneous insights and energies for growth and the healing of mind, body, and spirit. Each dream series demonstrates patterns of thought, emotion, and behavior that might be keeping the dreamer closed up, limited, and stuck. Each series also points toward patterns that might enable the dreamer to move into deeper self-knowledge and fuller self-realization. This book enables the reader to experience and appreciate the transformative and healing nature of dream work.

I am deeply touched by Rachel's courage and honesty in sharing the dreams and reflections that so clearly reveal the depths and heights of her own journey. She is truly a dedicated explorer who gives great honor to her dreams and to the healing power of dream work. *Dream Explorations* can serve not only as an inspiration to others, but also can serve as a guidebook for anyone who might choose to embark upon their own dream explorations, their own journey into self-knowledge and self-realization.

—Tallulah Lyons, M.Ed., author of *Dreams and Guided Imagery: Gifts for Transforming Illness and Crisis* and *Dream Prayers: Dreamwork as a Spiritual Path* and co-creator: IASD Health Care Project

PREFACE

Dreams have intrigued me for most of my life. In the early 1970s I faithfully recorded all I could remember for half a year, even though I had no idea what they were "saying" or that they could help me learn what my psyche considers important. Then during the next twenty years everyday activities of raising two children, becoming a professional artist, teaching art, painting and exhibiting took precedence.

I returned to recording dreams in the early 1990s. Attending my first dreamwork workshop in 1992, I was amazed to discover that one can understand the symbolism of dreams. I was just beginning to learn how to understand my dreams when I was diagnosed with breast cancer in 1994. The first dreams I remembered after receiving the diagnosis were a fascinating series of six dreams all one night. The first one seemed to state by means of metaphor what had already happened. It took many months, and in some cases years, for me to fully understand them all. I have recounted this experience in my first book, *Guided by Dreams: Breast Cancer, Dreams, and Transformation.* The illness and my efforts to understand what my dreams were trying to tell me about the illness and its causes and possible treatments became a powerful learning experience— part of my preparations for my life's purpose, helping others understand and learn about dreamwork.

Immediately after completing treatments for the cancer I attended the first of many dreamwork institutes and conferences led by nationally and internationally known dreamworkers, including Robert Johnson, Jeremy Taylor, Montague Ullman, Stanley Krippner, James Hollis, Marian Woodman, Paula Reeves, Murray Stein, Robert Hoss, and many others. I gained certification as a dreamwork facilitator through Jeremy Taylor's MIPD (Marin Institute for Projective Dream Work).

This book has come about as the result of reviewing the many decades of my dream journals along with the numerous articles I contributed over a period of eight years to a monthly Charlottesville (VA) area newspaper, *Echo,* and a national dream magazine, *Dream Network.* I began to realize what a wealth of information was available to me on a wide variety of topics. This information comes from deep within my psyche and is made visible through the symbols and metaphors in my dreams. The same type of information is available to you, the reader, when you study your own dreams. I hope my sharing of my story will inspire you to learn from your own dreams.

As we all know from experience, dream narratives can evaporate— escape our memory—if we don't write the dream down as soon as we wake up. Then, too, we often forget them even after writing them down unless we go back and reread them. Thus, periodic reviews of our dream journals are very valuable. During reviews we can look for series of dreams that deal with the same themes and images or similar circumstances to see whether we are stuck in possibly debilitating patterns of thoughts, beliefs, and habits or if our "positions" have shifted over the months or years allowing positive transformations. My discussions throughout the book are based on what series of dreams show about particular subjects.

Remembering how puzzled I felt about understanding dreams when I first began my study of dreams, I feel it might be helpful to show through my own dreams and some from my own family members how we can figure out their possible messages. I introduce various dreamwork concepts, terminology, and ways of "working" with and "honoring" dreams.

I am indebted to the many mentors from whom I've learned so much about dreamwork, through face to face contact at conferences and through the literally hundreds of dream books on my bookshelves that I have studied and still value. I refer to many I have found most helpful throughout the book.

Life is an interesting and at times challenging journey. As we set out, we may not know our destination or what roads or paths we should take. We often do not know or understand what we are meant to do with our lives—what our lives' purposes may be. It we can discover what is important to us, what talents we possess, we can learn how to prepare, then allow our lives to unfold as they are meant to. We can be helped along this journey by learning all we can about ourselves through the study of our dreams. I invite you to be open to this means of learning. Dreams can assist you greatly during your life journey in self-knowledge and self-realization.

DISCLAIMER

This book is not intended to replace or to be a substitute for appropriate medical or psychological counseling. Dreamwork as put forth in this book can be used complementarily to any medical or psychological care. Please avoid literal interpretation, particularly with dreams about disaster and disease. Unexpected issues and emotions may arise during various approaches to dreamwork. Please seek professional care for individual concerns. The author assumes no responsibility or liability for the actions of the reader.

—1—

INTRODUCTION: GOING WITHIN

How many of us live on the surface of life—going to work, doing our daily chores, interacting with co-workers, neighbors and family without being aware of what really matters most to us? Are we functioning on the same level we did a decade ago or have we matured and grown emotionally, mentally, psychologically, and spiritually? Is there any way we can learn more about ourselves without going to a psychiatrist or psychologist? The answer to the last question is "yes." We can learn a lot about ourselves by studying our dreams.

Our dreams come from a deep "inner knowing" within ourselves, the essential Self, the part of us that can connect our physical, mental, and spiritual bodies with the Divine Source, bringing into consciousness information and intuitive knowing that can help us grow and realize our full potential to become the "whole" persons we are meant to be.

Do we really want to know more about ourselves? I thought I did as I began a serious study of dreamwork. In one of my dreams early in 1992

I Decide Against Going Deep into Dark, Foreboding Woods

I am walking and come upon an area that is a meadow surrounded by woods. I think the area is beautiful and I walk some distance into the woods. If I were to go beyond a certain point it would become very dark and foreboding because it is too far from the opening where it is light. So I turn around, feeling it would be too dangerous to go farther, and head towards the opening.

Although I was not aware of this consciously at that time, the dream revealed I was fearful of delving too deeply into the unconscious. In the language of dreams, a collection of trees—the woods—often is a dream *symbol* representing one's unconscious. The term *symbol* refers to a tangible object or concept that stands for or suggests a deeper or more complex reality.

During the next seven years I attended many workshops and seminars led by nationally and internationally known dreamworkers and also read extensively. I wanted to become proficient in understanding dreams and to be able to help others explore their dreams.

Then in 1999 I had two dreams that showed I still had an unconscious fear of going within myself. These dreams spoke directly of going within. They used the metaphor of caves and going deep into the ground to represent going into the unconscious.

The Swiss psychiatrist Carl Jung tells us in *Memories, Dreams, Reflections* of the important dream he had of discovering a deep cave below the cellar of his house. For him, the cave represented a deep level of the unconscious and "the dream became for [him] a guiding image . . . ."

Exploration of a cave (the unconscious) can lead to greater self-knowledge. The first of these two dreams of mine pointed to going within something as part of my education. Even though I was in my sixties at the time, the dream used the image of going off to boarding school or college.

We're Expected to Go into a Deep Underground Place on Our Own

> I am being taken off to a strange boarding school or
> college by someone, perhaps my father. We enter a small
> building out in the middle of nowhere, which is to be
> my dorm. We go into a room that I will share with
> another girl. I wonder how I will get to classes. I don't
> have a car and this dorm is not anywhere near any other
> buildings. My father walks out, somewhat in a hurry,
> leaving me to my own devices. I notice that he seems to
> be fighting back tears—as if he hates to have to leave me
> in this situation.

I am not sure how we are to have our meals. Perhaps
we have a little kitchen. I have hardly had time to eat
when an unidentified man appears. He is to take us to
our "class." We are not taken to any classroom building.
Instead, we are outside in the wilds and are led through
rough terrain. At one point I discover what appears to
be the entrance to something deep in the ground. I have
the feeling we are expected to go into this on our own. I
stand by the entrance wondering what I should do. I'm
fearful and reluctant to go in—wondering if I'll be able
to get back out.

The action of my father in the dream was in keeping with what my
waking-life father valued, for he always encouraged me to learn and grow
intellectually, psychologically, and spiritually. But he died seven years
before I had this dream. Thus my father in the dream represented the
"wise old man" part of myself that realized the way to self-knowledge is
not easy; I may traverse "rough terrain" as I go to the place where I must
go deep within. However, "he" knows this is for the best. My ego (the "I"
in the dream) was fearful.

The second dream, occurring three months later, expressed my
unconscious fear of someone coming out of a cave.

We Fear the Person Coming Out of the Cave Might Be Threatening

My husband and I are walking outside and are passing
an entrance to a cave or a passageway deep into the
earth. I glance in, but then we hastily walk on because
we're fearful of being seen and followed by someone
who is coming out.

Even though I had been exploring dreams for many years by this time,
apparently a part of me still was not convinced it was safe to "go within."
Maybe I feared what the man coming out of the cave might represent—an
assertive, energetic masculine energy within myself. As I look back on this
dream now, I realize that this masculine energy could and would help

me undertake various new activities in the coming years. But at the time I had no idea how my life was evolving, and we humans often fear the unknown.

In 2001 a dream showed there had definitely been a shift within my psyche. Here is the dream:

I See a Woman in an Orange Dress Emerge from the Woods

I'm in an unidentified location with other people. We're in a wooded area beside a small body of water. I'm talking with others when I notice something orange in the water quite some distance away. I think I'm seeing an orange fish. Then I realize I'm seeing a reflection of the bright orange dress worn by a woman just coming into view as she emerges from a more densely wooded area by the water.

In this dream I saw a woman who represented a part of myself that had been deep in the woods—my unconscious—and was now coming into view in a dress—a symbol of an intuitive, feminine outlook. The color orange may indicate a blending of emotions and intellect, abundant energy, and a friendly, outgoing manner. I evidently was no longer fearful of going into my unconscious and was acquiring a greater understanding of myself. I had gained desirable attributes. The dream offered metaphors for gaining knowledge, achieving growth, making progress along life's journey toward wholeness.

A well-known therapist in the fields of psychology and psychoneuroimmunology, Paula Reeves, writes in her book *Heart Sense:* "Our dreams . . . urge us to discover who we truly are and what we must believe in order to be true to our core self." At several conferences I have heard her state: "When you don't know or care what matters most to you, that then becomes the matter with you." Our dreams are messages from our core self. From them we can learn what matters and what can contribute to a healthy future.

Even the most frightening dreams are coming to help us. If a dream points to a personal characteristic that is not flattering or a situation that is frightening, it does so to enable us to do something about it. As dream analyst Jeremy Taylor, co-founder of the International Association for the Study of Dreams, says, "All dreams speak a universal language and come in the service of health and wholeness. There is no such thing as a 'bad dream'—only dreams that sometimes take a dramatically negative form in order to grab our attention. No dream comes to say: Nyeah, nyeah, nyeah—you have these problems and you can't do anything about them!" Once we get the message from our dream, we can begin to act upon it in some appropriate way to help ourselves grow and mature into the persons we were meant to become.

Now after more than two decades spent learning how to explore dreams and sharing some of this knowledge by facilitating workshops, seminars, and small dream groups, I am convinced of the great value in dreamwork. I hope by sharing some of my experiences with dreams in this book I will inspire you, the reader, to begin to remember, record, and learn how to explore your own dreams. You will benefit greatly from this undertaking.

—2—

SELF-KNOWLEDGE THROUGH DREAMS

The study of dreams can be a valuable way to learn about oneself. Dreams come from deep within the unconscious and give us many levels of information. Some dreams literally delineate and analyze everyday occurrences, but many use symbols and metaphors to give us insights about ourselves and our relationships with others and our culture.

In dreams, we can be both the observer and the one observed and play multiple roles. Sometimes we are aware of this in the dream. However, in most dreams, the conscious ego simply observes and interacts with other people—either unidentified people or those we know in waking life. Many dreamworkers hold that all people, all creatures, and even inanimate objects in a dream represent some aspect of the dreamer. Therefore, by noting their characteristics we learn something about ourselves.

Can you recall a morning when you awoke from a disturbing or frightening dream? I imagine you were glad you were awake and it was just a dream. Can you imagine how you also might be thankful for having such a dream? You probably think I'm crazy for even suggesting this possibility. However, our dreammaker—an "inner knowing" within us that connects us with the Divine Source—gives us such dreams to tell us something it is important for us to know. Some people have told me they were afraid to study their dreams, afraid of what they might discover. But we need not be afraid. Even nightmares are coming to help us by making us aware of certain situations and suggesting ways to make improvements. Some dreams remind us of hidden talents. Jeremy Taylor, who has worked with dreams for over 40 years, assures us that we will remember the contents of disturbing dreams only when we are ready to deal with whatever the issue might be. We just need to figure out what the message is.

Nightmares often use images designed to shock the ego out of its complacency. In 1999 I had such a dream, one I found puzzling and disturbing:

I Observe Cannibalism

I'm out in the frozen landscape with others. I watch from several feet away as a scene unfolds. There is a woman lying flat. Another approaches, leans over and begins slicing off a section of the person's forehead, which seems somewhat larger than normal. As this is being done the forehead has the appearance of a large slab of meat. I wonder what in the world is happening. Then I realize *what is happening* as I watch the person begin to eat from the slice. Cannibalism! There has been no bleeding when the slicing occurred. I had thought the prone person was alive, but maybe not. That person must have been dead, perhaps frozen, and those remaining are trying to survive. I'm out there with them, although I seem to be just observing from a distance. Does this mean I, too, am in danger and will need to do likewise to survive?

John D. Goldhammer, in his book *Radical Dreaming: Use Your Dreams to Change Your Life,* recounts a similar dream of cannibalism. The dreamer tells of eating meat, which he noticed was the dead body of a man. Goldhammer explains that "[t]he dreamer lives on the money his deceased father left. . . . [H]e is unhappy because he wants to prove . . . that he is a useful member of society and is able to make his own living. In the dream, he literally lives off his dead father. . . . He has become a cannibal."

Goldhammer explains further that "when we turn our backs on our true potential, we are *choosing* to sacrifice our authentic lives, to allow self-destructive, societal influences to cannibalize the soul, devour our creative ideas, rip our authenticity to shreds."

In my dream, I—my ego, my conscious self—was observing other women eating a woman's flesh. These other women might represent certain aspects within me and also within women in general. My ego was observing women in our culture who have suppressed their creative expression and individuality as a means of survival. This might suggest the patriarchal atmosphere in which we exist. I then wondered if I, too, would have to do this to survive. As aspects of myself, the other women were doing this. The dream was bringing awareness into my consciousness. It invites me to ask myself how I was denying expression of my authentic creative self and why. Have I done so thinking it is my only means of survival? How can I change my beliefs and my actions to improve the situation? These questions can lead the way into the various stages of my journey towards wholeness, as they can for many people—both male and female.

Understanding one's dreams is often difficult. Because they speak to us through metaphors and symbols, they can seem very mysterious. Sometimes this is actually stated in the dreams, as in a dream I had in 1999.

I See a Monster and Other Strange Creatures In and Near an Old House

I'm outside an old house that is flanked on both sides with open space. The land on the right side slopes down hill and goes out of sight. I see a very strange-looking creature go way down the hillside. The creature was not anything I have ever seen before. It makes us think it's a monster of some kind. I go tell my husband, who is getting out of a car in front of the house, that some big mystery is going on and I want to find out what it is.

Next I'm inside the house looking out from a second floor window. I see a different creature come from beyond a house up the street. Later I see what appear to be small white objects the size and shape of irregular-shaped stones moving in a group, coming out of one of the rooms of this house. Then two men come out of the room. One sees me and speaks to me saying, "I see you have met - - - -," meaning the flat pile of "stones." As he says this, the stones take on a more plastic-looking form and the individual stones assemble themselves into a mask that moves on its own and actually speaks to me in response to the man's comment. I'm surprised and wonder what is going on. I feel the men have somehow created whatever this is.

Next I'm outside watching another strange "happening." A man is bending over an old-fashioned bathtub that is partially filled with various levels of a curving "plastic" substance. The man is molding what looks like part of an upper torso, and it is moving as if has "life" in it! What is this? Did the men create the "monster" I saw earlier? It was very large, as big as a gorilla!

A house in dreams is usually a metaphor for the dreamer. Men inside the house in a female's dream can represent attributes which we consider "masculine"—assertive, aggressive, outgoing, intellectual aspects. Carl Jung used the term *animus* to designate this archetype within a female's unconscious. The feminine attributes within a man are thought of as his *anima.*

Each of the tiny white stones might be a symbol for some small characteristic of my personality. These moved together and shaped themselves into a mask, that which hides my real self from others and maybe even from myself. I felt that the men, my "masculine" attributes, might be responsible for what was happening. What in my life could this be related to? What parts of myself was I obscuring—covering over— through my intellectual pursuits, assertive actions, etc.?

The man outside the house might refer to masculine influences outside of me. They seemed to be creating something "monstrous," something frightening to both my husband and myself. Perhaps my internal dreammaker was pointing out how a patriarchal society molds people into forms that appear monstrous to both of us.

I don't recall working on this dream when it occurred. But the fact that I chose the dream to discuss at this time probably indicates that it is important—for me and for the collective. In my opinion, overly aggressive, negative forces have been molding national and world events in an ever-increasing degree during the past two decades. Was my inner dreammaker trying to warn me, us, about this with this dream?

From a different perspective I might question whether this was true—that the creative force was outside myself. Perhaps "I" wanted to believe this to be the case. Perhaps they were simply truths I didn't want to face and projected onto others outside myself. It is possible for both perspectives to be true. They certainly are truths I might be frightened of, but need to face. Since the dream was bringing these into consciousness, I was ready to learn them.

—3—

WAYS TO LEARN MORE

I stated at the beginning of the last dream that I wanted to find out what was going on. How might I do this? Is there any way I might learn what the mask is saying? Yes, there are several ways. One way is to *incubate a dream*, asking as I prepare to go to sleep for one in which the mask will tell me its message again. However, the likelihood of receiving the desired response immediately is unpredictable.

Second, in a meditative state of consciousness, I can go back into the dream and engage the mask in conversation. I can ask it what it has come to teach me. Jung developed a process for this that he called *Active Imagination*. Detailed information on how to go about doing this can by found in Eugene Pascal's *Jung to Live By* and Robert Johnson's *Inner Work*.

Another process, devised by Robert Hoss and discussed in his book *Dream Language,* is a role-play technique he calls *image activation dreamwork*. While imagining that I am the mask, I can answer questions such as what is my purpose as the mask, what do I like and dislike about being a mask, what do I fear most about being a mask, and what do I desire the most? It is amazing how much this can reveal about what is going on in my unconscious that I will find helpful.

A fourth method of working with a dream by oneself is to *draw or paint the dream*. Stick figures and diagrams are fine. The visual associations that come to you while you draw and paint your dream may unlock startling "aha's" that would be difficult to access with verbal or bodily explorations.

We can draw these images from our dreams randomly on a rectangular sheet of paper or we can put them within a circular boundary, creating our own personal *mandalas*. In Sanskrit, *mandala* means "circle." The circle becomes a safe space in which our drawings can reflect and reveal the inner energies depicted in our dreams. By paying attention to the thoughts and emotions that arise while creating a mandala, we can become aware of important feelings and issues that need attention. This whole process can become a means of self-discovery, personal growth, and spiritual enrichment.

As we consider all the characters, actions, attitudes, perceptions, and feelings narrated in a dream story, we can ask ourselves how these are similar to or different from what is going on in our waking life and what we can learn from any similarity or difference. To help us recall pertinent information when exploring the dream in detail, as we write a dream into our journals or onto our computer, we should also include what I call "Day Notes"—brief notes about activities, thoughts, and feelings of the day we consider significant. We need to date them and give each one a title that reveals content. This will help facilitate later explorations and reviews.

We will gain the greatest benefit from dream explorations if we undertake the explorations shortly after the dreams occur. However, we do not always have time to do this. To be realistic, it is practically impossible to study every dream you have. Such an undertaking could occupy all your time.

Tips for Exploring a Dream

How do you know when a particular dream is important to explore and what parts of the dream you should pay particular attention to? It is logical that you will want to select the dreams that have elements that especially attract your attention. These might include ones that have weird, bizarre, provocative, "horrible," frightening, or "counterfactual" elements. Take note of your feelings—those in the dream and about the dream. If these are different, this could be significant. Look for recurring themes or images. These dreams will likely continue until you get their message. Notice and explore dreams that seem to be dealing with a major decision you need to make. If you are especially curious about a dream's meaning even though it has no weird or frightening imagery, it may be of particular value. Take note of any dialogue, quotations; they may be a special message to you.

If you are new to exploring dreams and are unfamiliar with the concept of images—people, animals, and objects—being symbols, you may ask: How can I know or learn what a particular image means, what it stands for? It is important to first ask yourself what personal associations you have to the image. If it is a person you know in waking life, what characteristics do you associate with this person? If it is a fictitious person, what characteristics are revealed in the dream? Is the person a thief, a liar, a helper, a teacher, etc.? If the image is an animal or an object, what are its characteristics? Every symbol reveals aspects of the dreamer.

If you know nothing about the image you can look it up in one or more dream dictionaries. I am cautious about which dream dictionaries I use. Some of those available in bookstores use definitions from the Victorian era, ones that most Jungian dreamworkers consider misleading or inadequate. Also, dictionaries will vary as to the number and types of suggestions they give. Thus, you may need to look in several dictionaries. Not all of the given possibilities will apply to your dream. Only those suggestions with which you resonate should be considered as possible interpretations.

You may next ask: How do I know an interpretation of a dream is right for me? Jungians agree that only the dreamer can say with any certainty what meanings his or her dream may have. This certainty usually comes in the form of a wordless "aha" of recognition. This "aha," a function of memory as Jeremy Taylor calls it, is the only reliable touchstone of dream work. Gillian Holloway in *The Complete Dream Book* lists numerous reactions you may experience upon hearing or reading a suggestion that may indicate the interpretation is accurate for you. She gives this condensed description of the "aha" of recognition: "This is part bodily sensation and part emotional recognition; some people say there is a sense of something clicking into place or a fog lifting as if someone had just washed the windows on your world."

One of the specific reactions Holloway lists is that you will "experience relief of some kind. Understanding your own dream is, after all, bringing information you already have in one part of your mind over into another part. In this sense, it's a big relief, like finally remembering the name of an actor or recalling where you left something."

Many years ago I had a series of very disturbing dreams. I was fortunate to be able to have one of them explored at one of the dream institutes I was attending. I was very anxious beforehand, worrying about the advisability of putting forth a particularly graphic dream. But since Jeremy Taylor was the guest expert for the weekend I had faith that it would be all right. My faith was justified. I was greatly relieved after gaining an understanding of the symbolism in the dream.

As both Taylor and Holloway suggest, our recognition of the correctness of a dream interpretation is a function of memory. But our "memory" can be prodded by ideas suggested by other people. This is the value of exploring dreams in a group. A member of the dream group I facilitated for many years in Charlottesville, Virginia, one day expressed gratitude for the many new ideas members of the group put forth about her dream. She said she had thought her dream very boring; she didn't think there was much to it and she almost apologized for presenting it. She was amazed at the depth of possibilities she now had to consider. Another member chimed in that she had learned through the several years she has been participating in the group not to discredit the value of any dream.

However, there will be many times when we do not experience an immediate "aha" of recognition. We may simply need more time to let various possibilities percolate in our consciousness. We may not have enough information; the dream is too short or our recall of it is inadequate. Or, if the dream is offering guidance of some sort as were some of my medical-related dreams, we need time to check out various options before we can feel confident we understand its meaning well enough to make any decisions based on the dream. However, if the dream seems to be a warning, we might consider whether some action is needed. If the dream is really precognitive, we won't know this until the predicted event happens.

There are many books available now on how to work with and understand your dreams. One of the more recent ones, Tallulah Lyons' book *Dreams and Guided Imagery: Gifts for Transforming Illness and Crisis* provides an interesting glimpse into how dream groups can work and gives detailed information on working with dreams. In *Negotiating the Inner Peace Treaty*, psychotherapist and dream worker Chelsea Wakefield explains how dreamwork can help you understand the archetypal energies that are at work deep within your psyche. Jeremy Taylor, in his book *The Wisdom of Your Dreams*, lists hints for working with your dreams yourself.

—4—

STUDYING DREAM SERIES

We can benefit from periodic reviews of our dream journals during which we look for series of dreams that deal with the same themes and images or similar circumstances. When we find some, we can see whether they reveal any "movement," change, perhaps transformation.

The following series of three dreams brought new insights to me during a six-year period beginning almost 20 years ago. The first one was in 1995.

I Need Peace and Quiet in Order to Get Things Done

> I am in the house of my family (parents, brother, cousin, etc.). Much activity is going on. People are coming and going. I'm in the midst of all the activity, trying to help, organize, and straighten out matters. I'm pleased when the rooms where all the activity is going on are cleared of people and there is peace and quiet. I feel that when this happens, I can accomplish some things, attend to business which needs to be done. But fairly quickly people come back in and things become hectic, making it difficult to do what I need to do.

On a literal level, this dream said I needed peace and quiet away from other people and the hustle and bustle of activities in order to accomplish what needed to be done. On the psychological level it was trying to tell me I was still operating from the standpoint of my upbringing—I was in the house of my family and was doing their business. I was in an early stage of my journey toward wholeness.

To fully understand a dream, one needs to consider what is going on in one's life at the time. Are there physical, emotional, or spiritual issues? In my case, this dream came one year after I was diagnosed with and treated for breast cancer and I was trying to understand possible causes for it and to learn ways of preventing a recurrence. Several doctors told me during the experience that I needed to nurture myself more. One theory says that women who spend considerable time and energy on caring for the needs of other people and neglecting their own may get breast cancer. Once aware of this need, I looked to my dreams for further insights, such as are seen in the above dream that pointed out a need for "my own space" for my own activities away from anyone else. I was not abandoning or rejecting other people, I simply need this for myself.

Six years later I had a dream that showed my psyche was living with the plight of many women who were dealing with breast cancer. It was about that time I began writing my book, *Guided by Dreams: Breast Cancer, Dreams, and Transformation,* about my experience. The dream stated:

I Lament Our Crowded Living Conditions

I'm living in some communal building where several people have to share the same space. It's very crowded and we lack privacy. On one occasion, I'm talking with another woman. We are lamenting our situation, saying we hope we'll be able to have our own rooms some day…

Actually this dream echoed one I had six years earlier around the same time as the above dream of needing peace and quiet. The dream was entitled *I Won't Stay in the Communal Living Space; I Need More Space and Privacy.* In this earlier dream I was refusing to stay in the communal living space; but I ended up there anyway. On one level these dreams spoke about my own individual needs. But I was sharing space in a "communal building." Thus, the dream pointed out I was sharing needs and concerns with other women. My first association was to other women who have had breast cancer. But it shouldn't be limited in this way. The dream addresses the needs and concerns of all women.

A few months later a dream considered space in another way:

I Search for My Assigned Space

> I'm wandering through the hallway of a public building, searching for a place to sit, or perhaps even to spend the night. It seems I have been assigned a place. I look past the door to my left, into what looks like a train compartment. I think this is my assigned space. I see an elderly man seated on one side. I decide to look farther. Looking through the next doorway, I see a much larger space that looks like a large hospital room. I watch as a hospital bed or gurney is rolled from my right towards the empty area to the left. I back out of there; I don't want to stay there. I may look farther, but end up coming back to my assigned space that looks slightly different when I return.
>
> The man has moved.

In this dream I was walking down a hallway (a place of transition), searching for my assigned place in a public building. (I was looking for my assigned role in life.) Since it was in a public building with one space looking like a train compartment, and a train is a means of transportation for the masses, perhaps this refers to the culturally assigned role for me—as an individual, and maybe in particular, as a woman. I didn't like the assigned place, which was also occupied by an elderly man. Not wanting to share the space, I searched farther. However, I certainly didn't want to stay in what appeared to be a hospital room (I don't want to be seriously ill again); I'd rather return to the assigned space. Perhaps it wouldn't be as problematical as I originally thought; the elderly man could be my inner "wise old man" (the wise masculine attributes within myself) who could help me. The space "looks slightly different when I return." I was beginning to change the way I see things, the way I think. This can be very transformative. Although "the man has moved" (these aspects of my inner being had changed position), he might still be there to share his wisdom with and through me.

Two months later I had this dream:

We Witness a Strange and Amazing Metamorphosis

> I discover a red spot on a surface, perhaps on water in a commode after I have used it. I become concerned, thinking it's blood, but while I'm looking at it, the spot enlarges slightly and begins to move around. I'm amazed to see that now it looks more like an ant. I go find someone to come look. As we both watch, this "thing" again changes shape and enlarges—developing wings. When it is the size of a moth, it flutters its wings and flies off. We have no idea what we have just witnessed.

In my dream, I witnessed a metamorphosis. I feared the blood signified a problem. However, blood is our life force, the visible presence of which often precedes a change, such as birth or death. In the context of this dream, I would say the change was a birthing of new possibilities, similar to that experienced by a caterpillar. This dream showed a definite shift in my psyche.

We can see when shifts take place in our lives either through specific dreams of rites of passage or through the study of dreams over a period of months or years—dream journal reviews. These will reveal where we are stuck, where changes are occurring, and what stage of our journey we are experiencing.

—5—

RELATIONSHIPS IN DREAMS

Most dreams deal with "relationships" on one or more levels. People in our dreams can be understood on both objective and subjective levels. Objectively, our dreams show what's going on in an external situation, how we interact with specific people in our waking lives; they bring into our awareness problems we may not consciously realize or want to admit. But when the people are not identified, these dreams can better be understood on the subjective level where all dream figures represent aspects of our own psyches.

Several concepts constructed by Swiss psychiatrist Carl Jung will help us understand these elements of our dreams. The first one we should consider is what he called our *shadow*—either *dark shadow* or *bright shadow*.

The Shadow

The dream in which I encounter and interact with someone, known or unknown, on one level can be pointing out my literal relationship to this other person. But on another level, the "I" in the dream represents my ego and the other person represents some aspect of myself of which I may not be conscious—and the dream is coming to make me aware of this aspect and the relationship of the attribute I associate with this person to my ego, my conscious awareness. Jung would refer to the other person as my *shadow*. He used the term *shadow* when dealing with characters of the same gender as the dreamer.

The term *shadow* is used to indicate the side of our personality that we do not consciously display in public or that we may not even be aware of.

It may be a part we have repressed because we consider it to be something "bad" (*dark shadow*), and we do not acknowledge or accept it. Our journey into wholeness involves integrating opposites within us—integrating what we consider "bad" with the "good." What we consider "bad" possesses positive energies we need to incorporate into our personalities.

Here are two examples:

1. What if you, a male, dream you witness a young boy murdering his father and you wake up with a feeling of relief? It would be understandable that you would not wish to acknowledge that you could be capable of killing someone. How can you find anything "good" in that? Remember the two characters are not to be taken literally. They are symbols; the young boy can represent young masculine energies within you and the father can represent old, worn out attitudes and beliefs. The murder can be the metaphor for eliminating limiting beliefs you acquired from your father as you grew up. Thus the dream might be suggesting that some beliefs that served you as a very young child are no longer needed as you mature and should be eliminated and replaced by more appropriately beneficial ones.

2. A woman might dream of some female who is rude and insensitive and does whatever she wishes without considering others' feelings or needs and without worrying about what other people might think of her. Such a character can be considered the female dreamer's *shadow*. The dreamer likely was taught as a child that a "good girl" is always polite and caring and does everything she can to help anyone in need; if she thinks only of herself she is being selfish. You might wonder how such a dream can be beneficial. However, if the dreamer has always put concerns of everyone else ahead of her own needs, the dream might be coming to tell her she needs to nurture herself more for her own health's sake.

In dreams the *shadow* is a metaphor for the most creative, exciting, and transformative part of the psyche. So it is very important to pay attention to the most disturbing part of the dream, which is likely to contain our *shadow*. We must first face and embrace the *dark shadow*. It takes a lot of energy to deny and to suppress this *shadow*. When we acknowledge it, embrace it, and release it, the energy becomes available for use in constructive ways.

Our *shadow* can also be a positive aspect (a *bright shadow*), perhaps a talent or creativity we don't realize we have, or a creative desire we suppressed as a child for some reason, maybe because we considered it belonged to someone else. It is also important to own the *bright shadow.* Sometimes this is even harder to accept than the *dark shadow.* But we each have something unique we can contribute in life. We need to acknowledge all shadow elements within ourselves and allow their positive energies to flourish for everyone's benefit.

Invitations to Integrate the Shadow

Often during the past two decades since I have been exploring dreams, Owen—my husband—has shared his unusual and sometimes alarming dreams with me so we can explore them together. Some of the seemingly most disturbing ones have led to great insights and have been very reassuring and encouraging once their messages have been understood. The following dream is an example:

I Feel Threatened by My Guide Through an Old Church

I am part of some sort of tour visiting old southern African-American rural churches. We are in a very plain, sparsely furnished old church, nothing much but the room itself, no evident pulpit, etc. A young, handsome, and articulate black man is serving as guide, at least for this building. He comments on yet another church building that he recalls in even poorer condition, that "didn't have any noise at all" or words to this effect, perhaps meaning neither preaching nor singing. I mention recalling a similar sort of situation. Other people leave the building. I start to leave also and he grabs and holds me and stands on my feet. He is very strong. He wants to have sex with me. He says, "We have to; we know each other too well." I am fearful and try to resist. I try to break away by forcefully striking him with my knees in the belly or crotch, which seems partly successful, but I sense I may not get away. Then I wake up.

My husband is a retired teacher and minister; he is neither a racist nor a homosexual. The dream was not dealing with either issue. So what could it mean? The color black often denotes the unknown and mysterious, especially when associated with fear or uncertainty. A dark-skinned person of the same sex in a light-skinned person's dream may represent the dark part of his personality, a part he doesn't want to face and accept. Whatever it is, we need to understand it, accept it, and integrate it into our beingness. It is a gift, the potential for wholeness. The sex act with someone is a union of the two people. It can be a symbol for integration, especially when the union is between black and white (opposites). Thus, the shadow figure in this dream was saying they already knew each other well and have to be integrated for the dreamer to become whole, to realize his full potential. The ego of the dreamer was exhibiting a common reaction to such a situation. The process of becoming conscious of our potential can feel threatening. We may resist the hard work involved on our way to wholeness. My husband needed to figure out what the dark figure represented and what positive energy it possessed that could help him continue to grow and mature. This might be determined by considering what characteristics the figure exhibited in the dream and/or what associations the dreamer has to him.

My husband also told of another dream:

I Feel Anxious and Remorseful about My Anger

It begins with my after-the-fact awareness that I have just had an episode of extreme rage, directed more-or-less specifically at a couple (man and woman) . . . . I have no recollection of what provoked the anger or of the incident itself. I can vaguely visualize the couple (middle-age, well-dressed, man with coat and tie and glasses, etc.), but do not know them in the dream or in real life. Apparently I did not do anything violent, except for the emotional and psychological impact on the people involved. I am talking with my wife about the incident, feeling very chagrined and worried, fearful that I may have caused real harm. . . . She speaks reassuringly about any possible harm, but I am still somewhat concerned.

Owen's dream came to bring into his awareness a deep internal rage, which he probably felt at some time in his waking life even if he has managed to keep it under control. In the dream the rage was directed at an unidentified couple. The rage very likely was directed at himself. Dream characters represent aspects of oneself and the description of the unidentified man fits Owen at the age he dreamed this. The female part of the couple might have represented his feminine aspects. The rage may have appeared as depression, which can be described as anger aimed at oneself. He was concerned about any detrimental impact his anger may have had on others. If it were my dream, I would endeavor to be mindful of my interactions with others and my judgmental attitude toward myself. I would allow into my psyche the reassurance offered by my nurturing, caring self, represented in the dream by my wife. Also, I would consciously seek to transform the negative energy of anger into a positive energy that can be used for good.

Relationship to Parents

By studying our dreams over a period of years and noting recurring themes and images, we may learn whether our basic approach to life— our thought patterns and attitudes—is changing for the better, is becoming more open to new ideas and possibilities, or is remaining in limiting patterns and narrow views of our early upbringing.

I was blessed with two very caring and wise parents whom I love dearly. Their love and wisdom were instrumental in guiding me into adulthood. My father lived to the age of 96. However, my mother was only 62 when she died. I regret that she did not get to see her grandchildren grow up and they did not get to know her. I will say more later about what her death has meant to me.

Even though my father was very loving and gave affirmations for my accomplishments, he had definite opinions—set views— regarding proper

In the dream I faced a situation that thwarted me and I managed to do okay. At first I looked to my parents, expecting them to take care of me. But I was able to arrange the necessary payment on my own; I no longer needed my father's help. This dream pointed out my growing sense of empowerment.

Still a week later the metaphor of the glasses returned.

I Become Anxious When I Don't Have My Own Glasses

> . . . I put on the glasses in my hand and they don't seem
> right. I look and they have heavy, awkward-looking
> rims, so I know they aren't mine. I become anxious.
> What's happened to mine? Where are they? . . .

Another year and a half later:

I Hand My Mother's Glasses Back to Her

> . . . I'm with my mother in some public place. . . . I
> decide I should have my glasses on, so I look for them.
> Someone shows me I have some glasses in my hands.
> They are my mother's, not mine. I take them to my
> mother and continue searching for my own. . . . As
> I cross the room I find my glasses on the floor in the
> middle of the room. . . .

This dream came two and a half years after the earlier one that mentioned my giving my father's glasses back to him. Even though my mother's death occurred 37 years prior to this, I seemed to be hanging on to/perhaps depending on her glasses, her views, longer than those of my father. The reason for this probably was multifaceted and complicated. I have grieved the loss of her presence for decades.

As I'm writing this, it has been 46 years since my mother died. This undoubtedly was one of the greatest losses my psyche has experienced. I grieve for the decades of missed opportunities to share so many experiences with her. Our daughter was only four and our son ten months old when she died. She would have loved to have known them as they grew into adulthood. I would have gained from sharing ideas on motherhood, creativity, and spirituality with her. This last has been shown repeatedly in my dreams. Upon reviewing and looking for dreams in which my mother appeared, I found a variety of significant ones. One of the earliest ones was recorded in 1992.

My Mother and I Attend a Concert

> I am to attend a concert of some kind and I think the
> whole family is going. Only my mother actually goes
> with me before it is to begin. When we arrive at the
> concert hall, she goes on inside while I wait outside for
> the rest of the family to appear. Finally I decide I should
> go on in and join my mother. No other family member
> is with her. We wait a little longer, then I decide I should
> go in the other door to see if they are there. When I
> go in, I notice that that part is divided from the other
> section by a wall and there is no stage. I do find Russell
> (son) there. I ask him if he wants to come join us in the
> other part. He declines, saying he prefers to stay where
> he is. I go back to join my mother. But when I get back
> she isn't there any longer. I stay for the concert, but am
> very upset and am grieving because no one else in the
> family has come. When I go out of the building I am
> still looking for the others and still crying.

At the time of this dream it had been 26 years since Mother's death. I was just beginning my serious exploration of dreams and I didn't know what this dream might mean. When I shared this dream with an intuitive counselor and author of several books on dreams, she asked me if I was the most spiritual member of the family. I said I didn't know—maybe—but that my husband was "seeking" spiritual insights also. She said she believed that my dream was an "actual visit" from my mother. The "concert" was "on the other side"—meaning in the spiritual world. My son was not in the same place with us. He was choosing not to join us at this time. I was upset because I wanted the rest of the family to share what I was learning and experiencing spiritually.

Someone else can give a dreamer suggestions as to possible meanings of a dream, but only the dreamer "knows," through an inner feeling of recognition (resonance) whether the suggestion is correct. I have experienced that "aha" of recognition. It seems highly possible to me that this could have been a brief visitation from my mother. The part of the "hall" where the "concert" took place represented the spiritual world where Mother came to visit with me. When our son, along with other family members, chose not to join us there, I was disappointed because I was (and am) eager for them to share what I was (am) learning and experiencing spiritually.

In the following dream, in 1998, I was seeking Mother:

I Have the Urgent Need to Find My Mother to See If She Is Okay

> I'm in a large old building—maybe a huge house. I
> walk down a long hallway. I'm experiencing uneasy
> feelings when suddenly I have the sensation of
> something poking or pulling at my back. I hurry on
> to my room. I become concerned and wonder where
> my mother is. I assume she is or has been there in the
> building. I have an urgent need to find her to see if she
> is okay. I begin searching for her and can't find her.
> I call out for her: "Mother! Mother!" very loudly—
> getting louder and shouting the second time. Others
> are aware of my actions and anxiety.

This dream showed how much I still missed her. Even though I managed to go about normal daily activities in a satisfactory way I still grieved deeply. Then four months later:

*I'm Horrified When My Young Daughter Finds
the Dead Body of My "Missing" Mother*

> I'm outside a home (maybe mine, but it's not identified).
> The area is very wooded. Some distance from where I'm

standing I see my young daughter (less than 10 years
old). She comes upon something stretched out on the
ground in a slight ravine. I realize it is the body of a
woman. Then to my horror I realize it is the body of
my mother, who has been "missing." I recognize her
hair—dark, stiff with lots of gray. The body is covered
with flowing folds of clothing material. I'm concerned
about the effect of this discovery upon the child. I'm
also worried that her younger brother might come down
a slight hill from a road above the ravine—and discover
what's there.

What a startling dream! The feelings I experienced in the dream were
those of great alarm and distress. I relate to this, imagining how I'd feel if
this were happening in waking life. I think it would be horrible for a child
younger than ten to discover a dead body, especially that of his or her
grandmother. But I need to remember the dream is symbolic. The setting
of the dream was a wooded area. So we can say the action was taking
place in my unconscious and my waking-life children represented my
own inner children. My ego—conscious awareness—was very concerned
about how these inner children (masculine and feminine) were or would
be affected by seeing the shrouded body. I wanted to shield them from
the reality of their grandmother's death, thus I was wanting to shield a
part of myself from accepting the reality and I continued to search for
my mother, as shown in a dream I had two months later—this time in a
nursing home.

My mother appeared in several dreams under a variety of circumstances
during the next four years. Then in June 2002:

*Alarmed, I Seek Help When My Mother's Car Becomes
Trapped in Vines and Tangled Branches*

I don't have any idea where this dream takes place. I
have been talking with a female—perhaps my mother
in the dream, but she doesn't seem quite like my
mother in waking life though. I can't remember what is

me. But there came a time when, although I thought she would continue with me, she was not able to do so. However, she had pointed to the path I should take. I can be thankful for the time she *was* with me and grateful for the loving guidance she and my father gave me.

Signs of Positive Growth

Exploring dreams is a way to discover whether we are making progress during our personal life journeys—whether problematical relationships with other people have evolved and been transformed, whether our inner attributes are becoming balanced, and whether we are realizing personal empowerment and fulfillment.

As symbols in dreams, plants—flowers, shrubs, and trees—can reveal much about our inner selves and our unconscious perception of the status of our personal growth. The health of a tree or other plants can mirror our psychological health. Planting new shrubs and flowers that flourish and grow in a dream is a very positive sign.

In 2001 I dreamed:

I Want to Put the Plant in My Own Area

> There is an area where flowers are placed or planted,
> which belongs communally to my extended family.
> Another area is mine alone. I'm given a plant that I want
> to put in my own area. I feel some of my family might
> think I should put it in the communal area, but I want
> to put it in my own area. I feel I have a right to do so.

This dream suggested that even though I wanted to do things for myself, I was still struggling with this issue of going against family opinion. But I sense I intended to allow myself to fulfill my own desires in this instance.

Roots may represent one's connection to one's family background and influences and cultural roots. I had a dream of finding a plant sprouting under a bed.

I Am Pulling Up a Long Root of Some Kind

> I notice short stems—or sprout-like protrusions—in an area under a bed frame. I grab one and begin pulling on it. It appears to be a long, viney root that keeps coming as I pull. I comment to someone with me that I hope it isn't a poison ivy root that I am holding.

By pulling on the viney root it appeared that I was trying to get to a root cause—something in my family background—that may be affecting a personal relationship. I hoped it wouldn't cause a reaction like poison ivy, which for me had been very bad in the past.

In still another dream I decided I didn't want to move to a new city to live with my parents. These dreams showed I was making the choice to be my own person.

Dreams about a Shared Concern

Our journey towards wholeness is an ongoing process. Where we are on this journey can be seen through relationships portrayed in our dreams. They can illustrate the bond and loving relationship between people and between people and animals. A husband and wife sometime dream about the same issues, as seen in the following two dreams:

Owen Must Decide for Himself

> I am with my husband, awaiting time for me to go on a trip. I am aware of how emotionally close we are and that he often senses what I think or feel without words being spoken. I want him to come over to me and be close to me while we wait. I'm not sure whether I want physical loving (sex) or just physical closeness. I sense that he knows or feels whatever it is and for some reason holds back from coming to me.

Later, when we're outside and I look off into the far distance and see a train coming, I feel the need to move to another area behind some kind of protective barrier between where I am and the path of the train. When I go there, my husband stays where we were. I very much want him to come over and be with me. I know that telepathically he is aware of this. I look towards where he is—longingly wanting him to come to me. I can only do this. I can't make him come. He must decide whether he will do this on his own. He has to want to. I am very pleased when I see him starting to make his way to me.

When I told Owen about this dream, he told me this dream he had the same night:

"To Be or Not to Be . . ."

We are in the house and I am at the point of death. It is not clear how or why. But we know I am terminally ill and will be dead in a matter of hours. I have a bottle of small pills about the size of aspirin tablets. Taking one of the pills will ease and perhaps hasten the dying process, but they are not intended to be suicide pills as such. To take one will ensure easy and non-traumatic death. My wife is supportive in this process, not at all distraught. She concurs with my judgment to go ahead and take the pill. So I do. But in the process of taking the pill I realize that I'm feeling relatively well and that perhaps I'm not really ready to die and have taken the pill prematurely. I raise the question whether the pill that I've taken will in fact kill me even if I change my mind about being ready to die. We discuss this. We discuss the possibility of my trying to throw the pill up. My wife appears ready to concur with whatever decision I make, but encourages the possibility of trying to get

the pill up and offers to help. I go to the bathroom by
myself and begin trying to induce vomiting. And then,
beginning to wake up, I realize I'm dreaming and I
don't have to do this.

Owen had these thoughts about his dream:

"The dream may indicate not a literal choice of physical death, but a
choice of whether to get up and make some creative efforts or go on looking
for diversion and palliatives that will in effect 'kill' the creative possibility.
I feel that this means in part that I have to make my own 'life and death'
decisions. And that while my wife is deeply caring and supportive she
properly cannot, should not, and will not make these for me. Therefore,
in the dream she did not try to prevent my decision to take the pill; and
she did not insist upon my change of mind after taking the pill, but did
offer support and help if that were my decision."

Amazingly, although the dream stories were different, the two dreams
had the same theme—he has to make his own choices in life; I can't make
them for him. We discussed the situation further, Owen saying that it
might be time for him to get counseling to help him work through various
problems. I was pleased; it was what I had been hoping for for some time.
But he had to make the decision himself.

Relationships with the Deceased Revealed in Dreams

Owen and I have enjoyed the love and companionship of pets all our lives.
My family had both cats and dogs, Owen's just dogs. We have had two
wonderful dogs and many cats during our many years together. Eleven
months after Cindy, our second dog, died, Owen had this dream, dealing
with his great sadness over her death.

Reunion with My Beloved Dog after Her Death

I am playing and roughhousing on the living room
carpet with our black Cocker Spaniel (who was
euthanized eleven months earlier, at age 16, because of
severe terminal disability). In the dream she is happy,

—6—

Aspects of Love in Dreams

We may experience love and sex in our dreams in a variety of ways. Our lover may be our waking-life partner, a relative, the next-door neighbor, our boss, or a complete stranger. The dreams may express our delight with a current situation, reveal our hopes for the future, or compensate for an unsatisfactory relationship. Some dreams may seem very strange or even threatening.

Carl Jung's concept of *anima/animus* can help us understand many of our dreams that speak of love, marriage, and sex.

Anima/Animus

When I—as a woman—dream of a man, in Jungian terminology he is called my *animus*, representing my "masculine" attributes. If I were a man dreaming of interaction with a female, the woman represents my *anima*.

What do you consider masculine or feminine attributes? Different individuals might list different attributes. But in general, masculine attributes could include being head-centered, assertive, aggressive, analytical, domineering, competitive, and knowing through logical thinking. Feminine attributes could include being heart-centered, receptive, emotional, tender, unfocused, indecisive, and knowing through feeling.

Do you feel that any of these are negative attributes? If you do, that's probably due to prior experiences within your family or community. A particular unpleasant trait of someone you knew may have dominated his/her personality, thus causing the trait to seem negative. In and of themselves they are neither good nor bad. Everyone has both feminine and masculine attributes. At times there may be competition within us between the masculine "doing" and the feminine "being." However, we need a good balance of the positive energies of both.

Heterosexual marriage in a dream, or simply kissing or having heterosexual sex in a dream, can symbolically represent the union of the masculine and the feminine within us. So, as a married woman, I might dream of being sexually attracted to some male other than my husband in a dream without it meaning I want to leave my marriage for whoever might come along. Let's see how this applies to some actual dreams, such as this one:

I'm Hoping to Marry My Lover

> I'm a young person in this dream. I'm physically
> attracted to a young man who initiates contact with me.
> I'm very pleased. We make love and I'm thinking we
> will plan to marry.

This is one of many similar dreams I have had through the years. Happily married, I do not have secret desires or fantasies of being with younger men. My husband has had similar dreams of being in the embrace of a radiant young woman. So what do these dreams mean? The "companions" in these dreams were unidentified, so the dreams were not discussing waking-life situations. The "companions" represented our animus and anima and the potential for an inner marriage—a union—of the masculine with the feminine. Knowing this, neither one of us became upset to learn we each had such dreams.

What might the following dream of Owen's be saying?

I Eagerly Anticipate a New Marriage

> I am eagerly awaiting the arrival of a young woman with
> whom I am in love. We are at least informally expecting
> to marry. She arrives, evidently by car, late in the day. I
> see her about 50 feet away and hurry to greet her. In the
> dim light she looks much like my wife as I first knew

her. My own age in the dream seems ambiguous. We
have a long, passionate embrace and kiss, and I feel very
happy. Then I see that she is accompanied by a young
man, slender, somewhat smaller than I, very blond,
fairly short hair, happy smile [myself as a teenager?]. She
and he are not themselves lovers or engaged, but I am
somehow aware that in marrying her I will be taking
him also. This seems odd, but does not disturb me.

Then later I am by myself reflecting on the prospect
of marrying the young woman and am thinking,
somewhat despairingly, that I cannot in good conscience
do so with all of the peculiarities and problems that I
have, things that, because of shame or fear, I never told
my wife about before we were married. It wouldn't be
fair to do that again. I wake up in this state of mind, but
with a pretty good feeling about the dream overall.

If you didn't already know differently, upon reading the first four sentences
you might think the dreamer was a young, unmarried man; but the
next two sentences rule out that conclusion. The dreamer is my husband,
an older man, happily married for many decades. Thus I consider this
dream to be revealing an inner psychological development of which he had
been unaware. My husband guessed that the young man might represent
himself as a teenager. The young woman very likely represented his inner
feminine, his anima. As I have already stated, in Jungian dreamwork a
dream marriage can signify an inner marriage, the uniting of a man's
masculine qualities with his unconscious psychological feminine aspects.

In his dream, when he married this young woman he would be
accepting the young man at the same time. What did this mean? Perhaps
he had "put aside" a part of himself as a teenager, which he would regain
by uniting with his inner feminine. This is why the presence of the young
man did not disturb him. The dream probably was coming to show him he
was ready to retrieve parts of himself he had either rejected or repressed and
to allow himself to express his feelings and to experience more feminine
attributes.

However, the dream revealed he had further concerns: he kept some aspects of himself—"peculiarities and problems"—secret from me before our marriage. He felt it would be unfair to do this again. Perhaps his acceptance of his teenage self showed he was coming to terms with what he considered peculiarities and problems. By the time he had this dream he had already shared his concerns with me. Perhaps he was still worried about them and the dream was bringing this to his conscious awareness. When he shared the dream with me, I was able to reassure him that he need not continue to worry. The fact that he had a good feeling in the dream was a positive sign.

On the literal level the following dream was an affirmation of my contentment with my marriage. On a different level it was another example of the coming together of the feminine and masculine elements within me.

I Approach and Embrace Owen

I undress and put on some simple wrap-around, sarong-type garment. I climb some steps up to a doorway through which I see a tall young man, my husband. He, also, is wearing a wrap-around garment, from his waist down. I deliberately proceed up the steps to where he is standing and we embrace.

Four months later I had a similar dream with a decided "twist" to it.

Owen and I Are Lying in Each Other's Arms with His Brother There With Us

My husband and I are very happily lying in each other's arms. There is another person, his brother (which he does not have in waking life) in the room with us. We know that he does not mind our being there together like this. We do not mind his being there either. I don't believe we are physically having sex, but we have a very warm, contented feeling about being together as we are.

For me this dream was neither a wish-fulfillment nor a compensation dream. My husband and I would never consider sharing our bedroom in this way. So why such a dream? To enable us to understand this and other difficult dreams, we must remember that our dreams often speak to us in metaphors. The inclusion of a brother, which my husband does not have in waking life, points to the use of metaphor. On one level, both men could represent masculine aspects of myself with which I had become comfortable. If I consider the dream on a semi-literal level, the brother might also represent a new aspect of my husband that I recognized and accepted and that I realized my husband was now able to accept.

Discussion of such a dream's meaning between a husband and wife can lead both to a better understanding of each other and their relationship; it did with us. However, you need to be cautious about sharing dreams in which you are having sex with someone other than your partner, or even dreams in which you are pleased by attention from someone else—perhaps an acquaintance or a celebrity. If your partner does not understand how dreams speak in metaphor, he or she might feel threatened or criticized. Sometime before Owen understood how dreams speak in symbol and metaphor his feelings were hurt when I recounted a dream in which I was enjoying dancing with a soap opera star. Since he was not a very good dancer, he felt the dream was being critical of him. However, metaphorically, dancing can be a symbol for moving in harmony with oneself and one's goals. Thus I was feeling at one with whatever the celebrity's characteristics represented within me.

According to Jeremy Taylor, we are archetypally predisposed to have sexual dreams that are related to our spiritual development. When sex appears unmasked, it is a symbol for something else. Sexual content dreams are projections showing what the dreamer's interior landscapes feel like. Things not sexual in dreams may be referring to something sexual. A few examples of this as given in one dream dictionary (*The Watkins Dictionary of Dreams* by Mario Reading) include:

- the insertion of a key into a lock
- the wielding of a stick
- the breaking down of a door by force
- the raising of a tower
- the entry of a train into a tunnel

As is the case with all dreams, the full meaning of such symbols depends upon the full content of the dream and the dreamer's circumstances in waking life.

Sometimes we may become concerned if we have a pleasurable sexual dream in which we make love with a family member, a neighbor or spouse of a friend, an animal, or even an inanimate object. We can relax and not worry if we will remember that all people, animals, and objects in a dream represent aspects of ourselves that need to be recognized, integrated, and loved. We simply need to figure out what this aspect is so we can bring it fully into consciousness.

Some people are afraid to remember dreams, afraid of strange dreams they think might reveal something terrible about themselves. Someone might consider the following dream to be such a dream:

A Romantic Alliance with a Female

I am in a romantic alliance with another female.
Somehow there is a triangular situation with a male
involved. Someone says to me that I won't be able
to have any child of my own with my alliance to
the female. I respond: "Yes, I can with artificial
insemination with the help of the male."

This dream might be a very normal and understandable literal dream for a lesbian. However, it could disturb a heterosexual woman. However, since dreams use symbols and metaphors, such a dream can signify a woman's recognition and acceptance of her own femininity, which the other woman represents. A child may represent some new, creative aspect of oneself, made possible in this context with the help of an inner masculine attribute, which the man represents.

A woman's *animus* may not always be helpful in the dream. Such a potential troublemaker would be referred to as a *negative animus*. Note the difference in the following dream:

I Discover My Suitor Is a Villain

I am a young girl in this dream. A young man who
seems very honest and friendly is showing an interest
in me. I'm flattered when he comes to see me. I like the
fact that others around me see that I'm being sought
after. . . . It becomes apparent that he is "courting" me
and that he wants to marry me. Someone shows me
that this young man isn't what he appears to be. The
person has discovered the fellow thinks I have money
and wants to marry me to get the money. When this
becomes known, the young man's demeanor and even
appearance changes into that of the "villain." He now
has darker hair and a very changed manner.

Marion Woodman states in *Conscious Femininity*: "Women . . . victimize
their own femininity with their inner masculinity. Their inner betrayal is
appallingly clear in dreams." In order for this new self-knowledge to be
helpful, I—the dreamer—needed to discover through careful introspection
what this inner aspect, this *negative animus*, was that could be detrimental.
Through careful dreamwork the negative can be transformed into positive
qualities and integrated into my consciousness.

Weddings

Dreams of weddings may come when one is preparing to be married and
can reveal one's anxieties concerning such. But when a person happily
married for many years dreams of an approaching marriage, what can this
mean? I repeatedly had such dreams. Those that announced a remarriage to
my husband showed my deep commitment to this relationship. But others
talked of marriage to someone different. At other times I was attending
or participating in someone else's wedding. Since all people in a dream
represent aspects of the dreamer, even when I was not the bride these dreams
were referring to the uniting of my feminine and masculine attributes.

Over a period of several months in 1992 I had various dreams that
discussed my preparations for a second wedding—one time the groom

was Owen; other times the groom was someone I did not know, had not known for very long, or did not know well.

I'm Marrying Someone I Hardly Know and It's Okay

> I seem to be the person who is about to be married. But I'm not sure (now and in the dream) who it is I'm about to marry. I evidently decide to get married to someone I don't really know well, but for some reasons (unknown) I decide I should do so. Afterwards, at first, I seem to be thinking I'll stay wherever I am, which is with my family, but I realize it is expected that I should go off somewhere with my new husband. I decide that it is the appropriate thing to do and I get ready (by packing some things). I decide this will give us a chance to get to know each other better. I may wonder somewhat at my marrying this person, but at the same time I feel this is okay. . . .

Why would I know so little about my potential groom? As already stated, symbolically, dreams of marriage are talking about uniting different aspects of oneself. For a woman, what we consider "masculine" attributes may be little known, perhaps mostly hidden, within her unconscious. Therefore, such dreams might be bringing knowledge of my potential into my consciousness, announcing it was time for an inner marriage, a union that would help bring psychological wholeness.

In another dream:

I'm Drawn to and Agree to Marry a Young Black Male with Great Healing Abilities

> I encounter a young black male who at first seems very threatening, but it turns out that he has great healing abilities, which he is using on me. . . . I am drawn to him and have agreed to marry him. I realize that others—probably my family included—will think this strange. I decide I should find out more about him and

45

begin asking him questions as he is administering his
healing skills. . . .

The color black often represents the unknown, the unconscious, the
unaccepted side of oneself. The important task for me was to learn more
about him, about unknown and/or unacceptable parts of myself. The
dream even stated he was a healer. How appropriate! The word "heal"
comes from the Old English word "hal," meaning "whole." Thus "to heal"
means to restore to health, to make whole. By getting acquainted with this
healer within and uniting with him, I would become whole. This is the
desired destination on our life's journey.

Several years later another dream of marrying a black man not only
showed the union of my animus and my feminine self, but also brought
in another issue.

I Decide to Marry a Black Man

I am with several unidentified people. I learn—or
know—that a man is either widowed or is being left
by his wife. I decide I will marry the man. Since he
is a black man I think to myself that this will "turn a
few heads"—or people will "take note" because of the
definite contrast in our skin color.

Later I am with this man in a public elevator, location is
unidentified. There are other people in the elevator with
us. But they evidently don't want to have anything to do
with us—or get near us. They all go to the other side of
the elevator and cause it to tilt precariously. I decide I or
"we" should get off the elevator because the situation is
very dangerous for everyone as it is.

This dream revealed the cultural landscape in which I grew up in the
South. Obviously I have memories of this that I can't remove even though
many of my family, friends, and acquaintances, and I have moved beyond
the attitudes conveyed in the memories. Some of the memories and feelings

may never completely leave us. My psyche was bringing this situation into my awareness again. Something may have happened around the time of the dream that triggered this. However, I didn't take note of it at the time and do not now remember what it might have been. My failure to explore the dream further at the time was a missed opportunity for growth. It was very likely I had a follow-up dream sometime that was attempting to bring the issue back into my awareness. I may have missed this also.

During these same months I was having additional dreams of marrying Owen.

It Seems Right to Marry Owen

> Owen and I are together, but not married. We are very drawn to each other. Somehow, as is very unclear as I try to remember the dream, we have had some "familiar" connection with each other in the past. We were not married, but had been associated in some family relationship that makes us wonder if it would be okay for us to marry. We decide it is okay and it feels very right for us to be together. We are very much in love and we plan to get married.

I have wondered if perhaps this was a reference to reincarnation; perhaps in a prior life we were related other than husband and wife. This could explain why we had the feeling of a prior connection. Regardless of what that connection might have been, we felt it was very right for us to be in love and together in this life. In waking life we do indeed feel we have a deep connection. When we first met we both experienced a special feeling, one that might be described as "a sense of recognition."

This next dream came about eight months before we celebrated our 40th wedding anniversary. Owen had one more year before he would fully retire from teaching.

I Announce to Owen We Will Be Remarried and Have Another Honeymoon

Owen and I are living and working in an unidentified
location. It is not anywhere we are or have been living
in waking life. We are married, but our life together
evidently is lacking any zest. There are many details
in the dream I can't recall, but I believe I announce to
Owen that we are to be remarried and have another
honeymoon. He is surprised and maybe questions
in his own mind whether I really mean it. I make
arrangements and tell him when and how it is to take
place. He is called out of his "classroom" and is told
details (which I can't remember now). I think the room
is to be our honeymoon room, therefore the regular
activities there have to be canceled or postponed. I'm
very excited about what's happening. I'm very happy and
sexually aroused. Owen is happily surprised.

The feeling tone of the dream was very positive. I woke up feeling good
about the dream. Since the last thing you would expect to be literal would
be for his classroom to become our honeymoon suite, I consider the dream
was metaphorical. It showed I was eagerly looking forward to Owen's full
retirement, when his concentration would no longer be in the classroom.
My dreammaker metaphorically was transforming the "classroom" space
into a "honeymoon" space, where we could renew our commitment to each
other and our "zest" for life could return.

A variety of dreams about marrying Owen and other kind, loving,
and supportive men continued during the next four years. Then came this
one:

I'm Getting Ready for My Third Wedding Ceremony

I'm getting ready for my wedding. It's my third. I'm
using the same dress I've worn—my waking-life
wedding gown—each time. I am repeating the vows
with the same person, my waking-life husband. I'm

evidently just renewing my vows. [After describing
many details of preparations, I recount that I am outside
after the wedding, viewing the scene as the observer/
witness to what's going on.] I see at least three women
dressed in wedding gowns. It dawns on me (as the
observer) that the wedding wasn't just mine. These
others were taking place, too. . . .

One possible meaning occurred to me. Perhaps the other three women in
gowns all represented aspects of myself. They represented my renewing my
wedding vows at each stage in my life up to the time of the dream, ten years
ago. I had just read in *The Circle of Life,* by Elizabeth Davis and Carol Leonard,
of the four basic aspects of women's life cycles: maiden, mother, matriarch, and
crone. At the time of this dream, I considered myself to be in the matriarchal
phase, leaning towards crone. In the dream, I might be observing myself
renewing my wedding vows at each stage in my life. On one level the dream
showed my continuing commitment to my marriage to, and love for, my
husband in waking life. On another it revealed the continuing union of my
inner masculine and inner feminine as I matured. I probably have become
aware of and incorporated new aspects at various stages of my life.

Two of Our Daughter's Dreams

Over a decade ago our daughter shared with us two dreams that seemed
strange or even bizarre. What took place in them couldn't possibly happen
in waking life. But by exploring the dreams, remembering they speak
a metaphorical language, we discovered they brought her a reassuring
message about a subject of great importance to her.

She was 40 years old when she had two dreams of going off a cliff or
the side of a mountain. Regarding the first dream, she recalled:

Mom and I Leap Off a Cliff

My mother and I leap off a cliff together. I'm frightened,
but Mom encourages me to relax and enjoy the
jump. . . .

Why would I, even in a dream, encourage such a dangerous act? You'd think we both would be killed in such a leap. The remainder of the dream explained why not:

> There is a current of air coming up under us that supports us and eases us safely to the ground. We go back to take the leap again. I have relaxed and enjoy the experience.

About a month later she dreamed:

I Take the Plunge Before Mark Does

> My friend Mark and I are together. He has a car that he intends to try out. But for some reason he decides not to. He offers me the opportunity to try it out. I accept and drive off in the car. I drive along curving mountain roads. I am both driving and seeing myself from above as I drive. As the car gets to a curve high up in the mountains, there is a waterfall and the car and I go over the edge and plunge down.

If this had occurred in waking life, she would have been killed. However, in the dream, she reported:

> Afterwards I am talking with people who are amazed that I survived and am okay. They ask me how it was that I didn't get hurt. I explain the secret. It had been prearranged that there was a transparent tube in the water that had air coming up which supported the car and let it down safely. The tube also protected me from the water.

In discussing the dream, Marcia revealed that Mark is a friend she palled around with. They used to go car shopping together. Not romantically interested in each other, they would lament that neither had a significant other. Then they each met someone, Mark first. Mark was now in a serious relationship with his girl friend, but not married. Marcia was to be married within two weeks after she dreamed this dream.

While trying to figure out the dream, it came to Marcia that the dream was saying it was safe "to take the plunge." She also wondered why Mark was in the dream. Then she realized that Mark had not married yet (he hadn't taken the plunge). In the dream he passed the opportunity to take the car out on to her, thus giving her the chance to take the plunge before he did.

Both dreams contained a visual pun illustrating the expression "taking the plunge" that we sometimes use when someone is getting married. Marcia felt reassured that it was safe for her to marry. What provided the safety factor? In both dreams, a current of air was providing the support for the safe descent. Let's explore why this is significant.

Rosemary Ellen Guiley in *Dreamwork for the Soul* writes: "The element of air represents mental effort, thoughts, intellectual pursuits, logic, and left-brain activities. . . . Air initiations often involve scaling the heights: going up a mountain (a spiritual ascent using the intellect). . . . In the mystery tradition, air is the third initiation and pertains to finding our inner strength and to attuning ourselves to always listen to the voice of spirit. Thus we are able to enter the temple of wisdom."

Sandra A. Thomson, in *Cloud Nine, A Dreamer's Dictionary,* gives additional information: "Air can symbolize inner/universal spirit; the creative 'breath of life'; your creative energy. . . . The Roman goddess Juno (female counterpart of Jupiter) was the personification of air. Identified with the Greek goddess Hera, she, likewise, was the queen of heaven, the protectress of women and of marriage."

In these dreams the air currents (spirit and/or thought forces) were uplifting and supportive. In the first dream Marcia and I knew that by prearrangement these means of support would be there for us. The bride-to-be wasn't at ease until she had experienced this support one time. In the second dream she evidently had no doubts. If these were my dreams, I would have felt very good about my forthcoming marriage. And she did. Upon hearing her dream, I felt rewarded to think that her dreammaker used me in her dream. This showed that deep down in her psyche she felt my presence represented helpful and encouraging feminine energies. By sharing such a dream with me, she gave me a precious gift.

Also, since all the people in a dream can represent aspects of the dreamer, on another level I represented the "mother" part of Marcia. In this case she felt it was a very positive feminine energy that supported and encouraged her. The dream was telling her she has these attributes within herself that would help her in her marriage and possible motherhood.

It is likely that Marcia didn't understand what the first dream was referring to until she had the follow-up dream. Sometimes a second dream is needed to help you understand a previous one. Both came to help her by giving reassurance that she was making a wise decision along her life's journey.

Marcia has now been married for more than a decade and is the mother of a bright pre-teen son. Thus, insights obtained from two very unusual dreams guided the soon-to-be-married woman towards very positive life experiences—a strong, healthy marriage and joyful and devoted motherhood.

—7—

HOUSES IN DREAMS

We choose where we live for a variety of reasons. We go where we find suitable and desirable jobs, to be near relatives, or to regions that offer activities or climates we desire. The houses we buy, rent, or build reveal much about our personalities and reflect our lifestyles and personal tastes.

A frequently occurring image in our dreams is that of a house. It might be the home we grew up in, a house we are planning to build, or a place we have never seen or thought of before. Sometimes the dream is not really about a particular house. Rather the house is a metaphor for the dreamer. The condition of the house, the part of the house we're in, and the circumstances surrounding it give us clues to its meaning in our dream. The house can represent our relationships at home or work, our attitudes, our emotional and mental states, and even our health.

A dream in which we are in the house where we grew up may relate to personal issues from our past—a troubled relationship with a family member or an old behavior pattern we need to change. The dream might remind us of a time we were especially happy or sad. We then can ask ourselves how are these issues or emotions relevant to our current waking life.

Renovation and New Construction

Many years ago I dreamed of visiting an old house to which I planned to move. This was not an actual house I knew in waking life. I have summarized the very long dream here:

Trips to Visit Our Future Home

We are there only to look around, not to stay at this time. It is a large, barny house. There is a lot of muck in the basement. On a second visit I find the basement still full of muck, mud, and silt—mess that needs to be cleaned out before the place is inhabitable. In the first visit a lot of furniture had been brought into the main part of the house and left. On a later return visit the furniture is still upstairs. I go down into the basement to inspect things. It evidently has been cleaned out some, but is still damp, not pleasant or livable. It needs to be worked on some more.

The large living room has a high ceiling and very tall windows, going all the way to the ceiling, with arched tops. The windows blanket the outside wall. The view includes a service station nearby. This is not very esthetically attractive, but I don't mind. It is a part of life.

The basement of a house often represents our unconscious mind. Also, just as the basement in waking life can be used for storage of a variety of items, a dream basement may be a psychological storage space.

The basement of the house in my dream was in bad shape. It needed to be cleaned before it would be inhabitable. It was not clear that I was referring to an old family home in this dream, but the implication is that I have stored away beliefs acquired in my earlier years. Thus, I needed to figure out which old thought patterns and past issues needed to be cleared away, what ways I could change my usual way of thinking, believing, and perceiving things that would be beneficial. Undoubtedly some of this would deal with my early unquestioning acceptance of parental rules and beliefs that some of the dreams discussed in Chapter 5 referred to. Three aspects of this dream encouraged me. First, I had been planning on this move. I was ready for change—looking to new, revised ideas and states of mind. Second, the living quarters had been furnished and were awaiting my arrival. Third, progress in the cleaning was evident.

The tall living room windows with arched tops letting in lots of light suggested much enlightenment was possible. The arched tops brought to mind the spiritual quality of cathedral windows. I didn't even mind the view of a service station (a symbol of help). I saw the service station through the window; thus, my outlook included a place where I could receive help or where I could be of service to others some day.

This dream came shortly after I had finished treatments for breast cancer. Many dream basements can reflect the health of the dreamer. Perhaps the dream was showing that my health was steadily improving at that time. It might also have been suggesting that a change in my beliefs and basic approach to certain aspects of my life could be therapeutic. This seemed to fit. Several people, including two doctors and a counselor, suggested this might be so.

On my last visit to the house I encountered a group of little old ladies holding an animated discussion in one of the rooms. They were so intent upon their business they paid little attention to me. I think they were "somewhat annoyed by my presence, but they don't tell me to leave. . . . I stand and watch. I feel I have intruded. Finally I thank them for letting me listen and I slip out."

I believe these women were my wise inner feminine council from whom I might learn needed lessons. My ego feared they were annoyed. But since they allowed me to stand and watch, I suspect they hoped I might learn something.

Four years later I had a dream in which

I'm Proudly Watching the Renovation of My Old House

I am watching construction work taking place in an enormous room in . . . an old place that needs renovation. A beautiful new floor (the symbol of our foundation and basic understanding) is being laid down in the living room in a specific pattern. I believe the person putting down this floor is a woman. The house belongs to me. Much activity is taking place. People are coming and going, some to do the work, others to see what is going on. I'm pleased with and proud of what is happening.

It was evident that progress was being made. With the help of the feminine aspects of myself, I was changing some basic concepts about myself and my life's purpose. My dreammaker pointed out more progress in the following dream:

The New House on an Old Vacation Lot Has a Good View

> I'm at a sea resort area. One house has been torn down
> so a new place can be built. It's near where my family
> had vacationed before in a house that is now gone. I'm
> in the new house talking with someone. I admire a
> wonderful view out a window. I say how glad I am that
> this new house has been built; the old house didn't allow
> for a view.

Houses can represent where we live mentally and emotionally. Our whole belief system may have been built upon the framework laid down in early childhood. In this dream the house my family and I used when I was a child was no longer there. Near the site a new house with a better view was built. This suggested that my outlook on life had changed for the better and I was pleased to see this.

Discovering New Rooms

In addition to renovating old houses and constructing new ones in dreams, we might simply be discovering new rooms in old houses. In one dream in March 1993 I was doing just that.

Discovering Many Upstairs Rooms in My Old House

> I am in the living room of an old house that I consider
> mine. . . . I go upstairs. When I do, I find that the place
> is enormous—with many, many rooms. It becomes a
> sort of old-fashioned hospital with winding corridors. I
> begin looking for my room, but I don't know where it is,
> I turn to the right as I am searching.

Six years later I was still discovering new rooms.

I Discover Spacious Rooms

I am in some very large house. I believe I'm living there, but I evidently haven't been there long—or at least I haven't thoroughly investigated the place. . . .

Still almost two years later:

Exploring My House

. . . . I'm exploring parts of the house that I haven't seen before. (Apparently I haven't been living here long. Logically, this doesn't make sense that I haven't seen the entire house yet.) I go through a hallway and an unfinished front section. . . . I seem to be giving instructions as to how I'd like this area finished off. I think to myself how this will make a lovely second "living room-family room" space. We already have a living room somewhere else in the house. . . . I go in and discover a very cozy, comfortable room that would make a very nice guest room or a "get-away" room for me, or whoever. I'm pleased to discover this space.

In another dream still two and one-half years later in 2001, I explored and discovered new additions and changes in our house and yard. New rooms and new spaces can represent all the unused talents you possess but were not aware of or that you suppressed for various reasons. They may include characteristics, beliefs, and attitudes that are being discovered or acknowledged. The type of room and its contents give clues to what they represent. The upstairs in the first of the three dreams discussed here "becomes a sort of old-fashioned hospital." This suggested my room—my space—was in a place of healing. The talents and transformed beliefs I would discover there could become means of "healing" in the true sense of the word.

they did not enjoy the brother-sister squabbles and we were disciplined accordingly. I have been interested to note how patient my daughter has been with her young son when he has been angry at some action he did not like. She has been open to listening to his reasons and then she explains to him her reasons. Even so, there *are* times angry outbursts must be contained.

I remember with regret an incident in my early adulthood, during my first year of motherhood, when I fussed at my mother, angrily accusing her of doing something I thought would "spoil" my infant daughter. Only later did I realize my outburst had really hurt my mother's feelings. This was a time I should have contained my anger. I was being unreasonable. My mother was only exhibiting grandmotherly love.

Would it be so bad for the rug to get burned, or would the opposite be true? In other words, did that part of me that gets abused, walked on, need to go? Did—and do—I need to express my anger rather than contain it? There are times, such as my thoughtless outburst described above, when my anger should be controlled. But there are other times, times when my rights are being jeopardized or I am being threatened, when I should speak up.

The "woman" in the dream represented a specific part of me; she can also represent "woman" in general. Thus this dream like many dreams can bring up the whole issue of cultural indoctrinations and women's rights. Society had taught me and women of my and my mother's generations that we shouldn't express our anger—we should think it not a problem when we contain it. Thus in the dream my mother didn't want to hear about or acknowledge a problem. But this is exactly why I had the dream. It was telling me to pay attention. There was something I, and other women of my generation, need to be aware of and do something about.

Ceilings and Basements and Fires

Another unusual series featured holes in ceilings with sometimes frightening scenarios. A ceiling can represent your mentality and its condition. Therefore, I can learn much about the state of my thinking by looking at these dreams. One dream in 1994 took place again in a basement.

Fire in the Center of the Ceiling

> I am in the basement of some very large building. . . .
> I'm in a very large room that may be circular with a
> domed ceiling. There is a fire on an upper floor in the
> building. Part of the ceiling, or maybe it's just water,
> begins to come down. I try to dash to one side to find
> an exit.

Fifty years earlier when I was a child, something similar happened to my father. He and another man were fighting a small fire with a fire extinguisher in the center of a circular room. My father had just started to the door to get more help when the ceiling gave way. He escaped; the other man didn't. Our unconscious sometimes uses images from our conscious experience in our dreams. Usually the events are recent; but in this case, my dreammaker pulled a very traumatic event from the distant past, perhaps knowing I would take special note of such a dream.

Plaster falling from the ceiling might show a possible need to change one's beliefs. Water coming through the ceiling might suggest being flooded with emotion. This makes sense. I know I would get emotional if there's a fire in the building above me and I would dash to find an exit. We consider fire to be a destroyer, but it also purifies and transforms. The forest service often deliberately burns an area to get rid of old, perhaps decaying trees to allow for new growth. Thus, the fire along with the falling plaster in this dream might suggest the possibility that a way was being opened to allow new thoughts into consciousness.

This dream took place in the basement, which can represent our unconscious. This is fitting, since dreams are messages from our unconscious. In fact, one of my dreams simply stated I had gone down into a basement to get information.

During the six months preceding this dream, I was diagnosed with and treated for breast cancer. As I describe in *Guided by Dreams*, I feel the whole cancer experience was a wake-up call—a life-transforming event—through which I received guidance from my inner or Higher Self. The experience was very anxiety producing and caused me to give much thought to the meaning of my life and the direction I wanted it to go in the future—what I need to do as I continue my journey toward wholeness.

In the above dream, my dreammaker was using a very traumatic event similar to one from my childhood to suggest that the experience and trauma of my illness could lead to something good—to transformation and a new direction for my future.

Two years later I had another "ceiling" dream:

Hole in the Ceiling Knocked Out to Let in Light

Visiting some unidentified place, we are going from one part of the building where we are staying into another part, maybe a kitchen or family room that is fairly dark. There may be only one window. What is surprising is that there has been a section of the ceiling knocked out to let in light. The man of the house is sitting in the room drinking some beverage. He thinks nothing is unusual about the situation.

A kitchen is the room in which food is stored, then prepared for consumption. Food can be food for thought. The one window in this kitchen didn't provide much light with which to see, understand, and receive available food for thought.

In the dream I was surprised to see that a section of the ceiling had been knocked out to let in light. A way had been provided to let in more light/insight into the room. Therefore, I would more easily be able to receive food for thought that I might sometime share with others.

"The man of the house"—my animus—was calmly drinking a beverage as if nothing was unusual about the situation. He was comfortable with this situation. I would guess he was responsible for the hole in the ceiling. What about his beverage? If it was alcohol/spirits, according to Carl Jung it might symbolize seeking connection with the divine. If it was plain water, it might more simply symbolize quenching your spiritual thirst.

These dreams related unusual, fictitious experiences, although one seemed based on a very traumatic childhood memory. I believe they were meant to show me metaphorically that my life is going in the right direction.

A year later, in 1999, I was delving deeply into the study of dreams, attending workshops and dream institutes. This next dream reflected this:

My Dorm Room Is Very Spacious and Has Lots of Light

> I'm in a dorm at some institution where I plan to take classes. My room is very spacious with large expanses of windows on the end and part way on each side. At some later point I'm talking with either my husband, brother, or friend, exclaiming over how wonderful the space and windows are. He comments on how it is as light as my place back home.

In the dream I was exclaiming over my spacious room with expansive windows at an institution for learning. My animus, represented by my male companion, compared it favorably to the amount of light I had at home. Recall that I was appreciating all the light that would be let in through the tall living room windows in the first dream at the beginning of this chapter. Thus, several dreams over a span of five years proclaimed the virtue of letting in as much light/insight as possible.

—8—

BATHROOM DREAMS

Bathrooms are special, needed features in houses. Since dreams of bathrooms make up one of the most common categories of dream themes and one I have had frequently through the years, I think it merits a separate chapter.

Bathroom dreams can deal with our natural process of elimination—"going to the bathroom." We are likely to be reluctant to discuss the subject. Such dreams may be the result of physical stimuli, but they can also be metaphors for unconscious needs that are trying to come into our consciousness.

We use the bathroom to cleanse our outer bodies and to clear out wastes from our interiors. In dreams, these actions may symbolize the releasing of tensions and emotions, the clearing away of old habits and beliefs, and the elimination of what no longer contributes towards our health and wholeness. The process of elimination can also be a metaphor for expressing ourselves, telling others of our feelings and ideas.

It is helpful to pay attention to the particular circumstances of our "bathroom" dreams:

- Where are they taking place?
- Are the facilities what you expect to find or different?
- Do you have privacy? If you don't, how do you feel about this?
- Do you have trouble finding a bathroom?

For more than three decades I have recorded many dreams of searching for a bathroom. Many times I could not find one. When we find no place "to go," this might symbolize our inability to find a way to release our tensions and let go of hurts, habits, and outdated beliefs. It might also suggest we are not finding a way to express ourselves—to share our thoughts and feelings with other people or to give expression to our creativity.

In 1994 I had the following dream:

There's No Bathroom Available in Area Where Women Are Allowed

> I'm with a small group of people going to a building
> and going to a particular place— lounge—gathering
> room—on a lower than ground floor level. I think we
> just go to talk. Don't believe we eat. We seem to be
> confined to just one particular area. When I announce I
> need to use the bathroom I'm told I can't use any there,
> that women aren't allowed beyond the room we're in in
> that building. So we get up and leave.

Rosemary Guiley states in *Dreamspeak*: "Urination often relates to creativity—something that flows forth from within. When we release creativity, sometimes we are surprised at how much we have within us. . . . Defecation also can relate to creativity—it is something solid that issues forth from the center of your being." When we pay attention to the circumstances in the dream, they may show us how and where we are being blocked or not allowed expression and creativity.

With this dream I need to ask myself:

- Under what circumstances in waking life was I being kept from expressing my needs and feelings?
- Was I having to hide my emotions and/or fears?
- Was I searching for ways to share my talents with others?

In another dream I located the women's bathroom in a small public building but found "a sign has been posted. It's no longer a bathroom. The space is being converted for some other use. Carpenters are working on it now." I considered slipping into the men's room, but I could tell it was in use, so I decided I couldn't use it.

Two years later, in a dream this happened again:

I Tell the Males to Wait

> Evidently this is the only bathroom for both males and
> females. The males are angered because I'm there and
> they can't come on in. I tell them I'll be out shortly and
> then they can come in. They back out and have to wait.

In thinking about this, I had a sense of satisfaction that I stood up to them
for my right to be there.

There was a dream in 1997 that began with my having to ask permission
of the man I was with to use the commode.

I Ask the Man If I May Use the Commode

> I am in a strange hotel room. First I seem to be with my
> husband. But then I'm with a strange man, someone I
> do not know—in waking life and in the dream. I need
> the bathroom. I ask the man if we have a commode in
> our room. There is a door off one corner of the room.
> I had assumed there is a bathroom there. The man
> is standing up, maybe looking into a mirror near the
> corner. He moves aside and reveals a commode in the
> corner. I think to myself that I hadn't seen it because the
> door to the adjoining space covered it when it was open.
> I ask the man if I may use the commode. He is standing
> near it and will have to move out of the way if I'm to use
> it. He says it's okay and moves. . . .

This dream was discussed at an Institute for the Enhancement of Dreamwork
weekend some months later when Jeremy Taylor was the guest facilitator.
He pointed out that this part of the dream was about the lack of ability to
have free authentic expression and that the rest of the long, complicated
dream dealt with the consequences of not having free expression. I discuss
this in more detail in Chapter 22.

Then in a dream in 2001, when I heard a woman asking for permission to go to the bathroom,

I Think the Woman Should Not Need to Ask Permission

> I'm sharing a bedroom with several other women. At one point during the night I see one get up. I overhear her ask someone (unidentified), rather timidly, if she may go to the bathroom. She receives permission. I think to myself that she should just go. No need to ask permission.

Since the other woman might represent some aspect of myself that still felt the need to be submissive, I am encouraged to see that the need to be more assertive was coming into my consciousness.

Back in 1991, I had a dream that showed my sentiment towards men who tried to take advantage of me—a woman—while I used an outdoor facility.

The Bathroom Facility Is a Long Shaft with Men Below

> . . . Early, in this dream, I am in some strange area (details have escaped me now). I need to use the bathroom and am shown to some place—the only place where there is a bathroom and the only type of bathroom facility existing. I go into the space and sit down on the facility, only to become aware that it is a very exposed place—below the seat I am sitting on there seems to be a long, open shaft. There are several male persons down below taking advantage of the situation, looking up to see what they might see. Somewhat worried and concerned to begin with, I decide that I will go ahead and use the facility anyway. It will be just their tough luck if that is what they are going to be doing. If they are in the way below, tough luck. . . .

Obviously I didn't like the situation, but I felt that the men would be getting what they deserved. I have no recall of what waking-life circumstances might have triggered such a dream. The sentiment and action suggested in the dream would have been a negative means of being assertive. As subsequent bathroom dreams already discussed showed, it took me several more years to become consciously aware of being assertive in a positive manner.

In some bathroom dreams we may find ourselves "going" in full view of other people in various situations. The titles I gave the dreams often told the essence of their stories. These included *I Have Trouble Finding Privacy to Go to the Bathroom.*

In some dreams, when ordinary bathrooms were not available, I "went" in some very strange and very public places. Such places included the middle of a receptionist's office and a very public passageway. Were these dreams suggesting that I was expressing myself —venting my emotions and/or telling my views—in places where it was inappropriate? Or did my upbringing make me think this was the case and the dreammaker wanted me to become aware of this so I could rethink and re-evaluate the situations?

One of the most unusual bathroom dreams occurred early in 1997.

I Have to Use an Attic Bathroom with Holes in the Floor

I am entering a large room, maybe a dining room, where
I'm supposed to sit in a special place—as an honored
guest or to receive an honor. Before going to my place I
need the bathroom. I ask where one is and am told there
is not one there. I have to go out looking elsewhere. I
find a very large attic with holes in the floor—which
evidently is being used as a bathroom. I go use a hole
that is to one side by the wall. While there, I watch,
observe other females and males. The females squat.
The males partially squat or kneel, so as to not be too
exposed. Afterwards I want to wash my hands. There is
nowhere there to do this. I ask where I can wash and am
shown a tiny "phone booth-type" place where I have to

reach in to wash. As I return to the dining room I see
that there is a small bathroom off to the right of where
I'm to go. I should have been shown this. I'm slightly
upset that I was denied the use of this more convenient
and better place.

When we have these types of dreams we can ask ourselves various questions,
such as: In the dream, did we feel comfortable in such situations or did
we feel the need for privacy? What in our personal lives has the same
feel? What was going on in our waking life that might have triggered the
dream? Do we feel our opinions are not wanted—would not be appreciated
if we express them? Do we feel our jobs are uninteresting and do not allow
us to express our talents and creativity?

Another very unusual dream is this one I had in 1999:

Women Fear I'll Throw the Bathroom Off Balance If I Climb on Up to It

I am in an unfamiliar place and I need the bathroom.
I ask someone where I may find one. I'm told that
there is a way nearby that leads to one which is on an
upper floor. But something about getting there may be
difficult. I don't remember what was said. Then I'm told
there is another way through a doorway in a building
just a little way beyond. So I decide to go that way. After
going through that door I discover the facility is not
right there. I have to wind through hallways and up to
a floor above. Then when I'm almost to the bathroom
I find that there is a type of ladder stairway up to the
door of the bathroom. I begin to climb this. Part way
up I see that the door to the bathroom is open and I
now see there are several women there waiting to use the
facilities. As I begin to climb another rung on the ladder
the place begins to move as if my climbing further up
will throw the room off balance. The women become
alarmed and tell me not to come on up. At this point I
notice that there is a stairway to my left that evidently

comes up from ground level below. I assume that this
was the first way up I was told about. I believe I decide
just to go back down that way. The women in the
bathroom above don't want me to come on up since I'll
"rock the boat" too much.

I think this dream was pointing out that the way to get to a place for
self-expression was very difficult. And when I had almost reached the
destination, other women there didn't want me to come on because doing
so would "rock the boat." What was I doing in waking life that "rocked
someone's boat"—might throw them off base? Did the other women
represent parts of myself that feared my success? Did this hold me back as
it did in the dream—or did I succeed in spite of doubts?

In dreams, the process of elimination may also symbolize getting rid of
something that has lost its value or needs to be flushed away. Another dream
in the "initial dream series" after my breast cancer diagnosis symbolized
flushing out toxins from within my body. Here is the dream:

I Dump Excrement into a Man's Cap

I am carrying a container that has excrement in it. I'm
not sure whether it is mine or somehow I have collected
or picked up some. Anyhow, I am looking around
(outside on open ground) for a place to get rid of it. I
see something that looks like a small container on the
ground, so I dump the stuff in there. I am surprised
to see some man come along looking around on the
ground. He seems to touch this object with his lip or
mouth as if testing to see if it is what he is looking for.
The idea of his doing this repulses me. I certainly think
this is strange. He then picks it up and I am either told
or realize somehow that the container is his cap. I am
very alarmed that I had dumped the shit into it. I think
I am apologetic and try to explain what I had done, not
realizing the container was a hat. The man doesn't seem
concerned. A crowd of people who are around and have

seen what is happening actually laugh and/or snicker at
the whole incident.

Excrement is a waste product from the body, composed of things no longer needed and/or toxins. Inability—in waking life—to get rid of such can lead to physical illness. In the dream, the excrement could have been referring to actual lingering cancer cells that needed to be eliminated or it could have been a symbol for a variety of irritants, negative characteristics, and undesirable aspects of myself that needed to be eliminated. These might include negative thoughts and feelings, old hurts, or old habits.

It's interesting to note that "I"—the ego in the dream—was reluctant to claim the excrement as my own. I was ashamed to think it (and what it represented) might be mine. I was also repulsed to think the man had put it to his mouth or lip. Who was this man? On one level he might represent the pathologist who ran the test to check for cancer. But since I thought his actions strange (and I wouldn't label a pathologist's actions strange), it is likely there was an important, deeper meaning. I had put the excrement in his cap—perhaps his "thinking cap." Maybe my dreammaker thought this appropriate as a receptacle for negative feelings and thoughts. By his actions the man—my animus—affirmed that getting rid of the "stuff" was good and he would help me to do it. The crowd of people represented the many extraneous parts of myself that were embarrassed by the whole situation. Snickering is often a sign of embarrassment. The man was not offended and I should not be ashamed or embarrassed. Remember this dream was part of the "initial dream series." So I was being given advice regarding what I needed to do to "heal" right from the beginning.

—9—

THE BODY AND HOW IT IS CLOTHED IN DREAMS

Dreams that deal with our bodies come in many forms. Sometimes the body part is specifically mentioned. Other times other things, such as houses, cars, and our pets, are used as symbols to represent our bodies. When this is the case we may learn of problems in our bodies by noticing the condition of the house or car or particular parts of each. For instance:

- A plumbing problem in a house may symbolize a digestive tract problem.
- A faulty pump might represent a heart problem.
- If a car has headlights that don't work, the dreamer may have eye problems.
- If the gasoline won't feed properly, there may be a problem with assimilating food.

Many of these are common sense metaphors. If you are just beginning the study of dreams, you might like to read some discussions on body symbols. Penny Pierce's *Dreams for Dummies* has a good section on these kinds of symbols and Patricia Garfield has an excellent discussion in her book, *The Universal Dream Key*. I give a personal example, one in which a pet with a problem was trying to warn me of a potential illness, in Chapter 19, *Healing Through Dreamwork*. This later chapter includes additional examples of prodromal dreams—dreams in which symptoms of illness seem to appear prior to their arrival in waking life. The words *prodromal* and *prodromic* come from the Greek word *prodromos*, meaning "running before." While we are more familiar with the term *precognitive* relating to knowledge of an event or state not yet experienced, the words *prodromal* and *prodromic* relate specifically to symptoms of disease.

Wilda B. Tanner in *The Mystical, Magical, Marvelous World of Dreams* reminds us, "From ancient times the various parts of our bodies have been symbolically linked with definite meanings. These correlations are well-known and understood at the subconscious level of our minds, even though we no longer have a conscious knowledge of them." Since our dreams come from our unconscious, they are bringing into consciousness this information.

We also hint at such meanings in the idioms we use in our everyday language. Here are a few we use frequently mentioning eyes and sight, feet, and hair: "I see," "you must be blind," "keep your eyes open," "looking through rose-colored glasses," "keep your feet on the ground," "you have feet of clay," "put your foot down," "a hair-raising event," "make your hair stand on end," "and "let your hair down."

Here's a dream I had in which I felt I had "feet of clay":

My Feet of Clay

> I am going to a meeting of a group I want to participate
> in. I ask if it is all right for me to come in. I feel they
> may not want me because I have thick cakes of mud
> on my feet, which are bare. Mud is caked between my
> toes. As I point this out, the person in charge says it's
> okay; I'm welcome anyway. He points to the next person
> behind me, showing me that this person also has bare
> feet covered with clay. We are both welcome.

In this dream I felt insecure, inadequate, and unsure of being welcome because of the feet covered with clay. Though the feet are not literally made of clay, the image is that of "feet of clay." We often use this expression to suggest a person has a hidden flaw or weakness. It is interesting to note that the expression comes from a story in the biblical Book of Daniel about King Nebuchadnezzar's dream of a massive statue constructed of various precious metals. The problem

development and growth. By noticing this about my dreams, I can remain cognizant of how I am progressing on my life's journey.

Teeth Dreams

Another common dream theme for me, and many people, has teeth crumbling and falling out. I first recorded one of these forty years ago.

My Teeth Crumble

My teeth are crumbling in my mouth. As this happens I am instructed by someone (don't know who) to save the bits of teeth and even the powdery teeth to take to the dentist to be reworked and put back in place. I remember saving the bits and crumbs of teeth as the teeth begin to crumble. I save the matter in a tissue, napkin, or something similar.

Then twenty years later:

My Teeth Are Crumbling While I'm Teaching an Art Class

I'm teaching an art course to a group of people. . . . While I am teaching, my teeth begin to crumble very badly. I am catching the pieces of teeth in my hands as I spit them out. I realize I need to go to a dentist right away. I go . . . looking for help. I see some nurses and ask them if there is a dentist here. I say I am in bad need of help and I probably show them the crumbled teeth in my hands. But there is no dentist here.

It is commonly thought that losing one's teeth indicates a problem. On a literal level, you should check to see if you have an actual problem with your teeth. But on the psychological level, dreams of teeth falling out might represent feelings of loss of power or control, a sense of insecurity and inadequacy. What aspect of my life feels as if it is falling apart, crumbling?

To explore this last dream further, I need to look back through my journals to see what was going on in my life at the time of the dream. This is why recording "Day Notes"—activities, thoughts, and feelings of the day—is valuable. I don't always understand my dreams when I have them. Sometimes a dream may foretell something that will take place in the future. Other times later dreams will give us further clues regarding the meanings.

Clothing

Clothing, the way we dress, often plays a significant role in our dreams. In our waking lives we often are concerned about what we wear. We want to dress appropriately for what we are doing. Sometimes we might want to impress someone with what we are wearing. Our outer appearance, our image, how we look to others is created by our clothing. Thus, in dreams, clothing may be a symbol for how we present ourselves to others. It may also represent attitudes, ideas, and emotions we feel or "put on." The psychologist Carl Jung called this our *persona*.

While reviewing my dreams beginning in the mid-1990s, I discovered a series that mentioned clothing. The first one I'll describe occurred not long after I attended my first weeklong Dream Conference at Kanuga (a conference center near Hendersonville, North Carolina). My dreammaker used the setting of a conference for this dream:

Attending a Conference Where Everyone Wears the Same Kind of Jacket

> At a conference I am climbing up to my seat in what appears to be bleacher-like seats and I am carrying packages that make rustling, crackling noises. I remember wearing some particular type of jacket or coat that is like or similar to those other people are wearing. I had noticed other people wearing them. I thought they were attractive and special, but maybe expensive. I may be surprised to realize I am wearing one, too. Then I seem to realize it is common for those attending this conference.

In this dream I noticed that many of the participants at the conference were wearing the same type of jacket or coat. This suggested that many people there had the same or similar ideas and attitudes. This seems fitting to me as I reflect upon this. I assume that many people attending such a dream conference would be entertaining many of the same ideas. We were learning the same material regarding working with dreams. In the dream I was surprised to see I had on a similar jacket. I should not have been surprised. I labeled the jackets as "attractive and special." I would say this is how I felt about the new ideas I was learning at the conference in waking life.

The following "clothing" dream, which came almost four years later, pointed out the need to give careful thought to which groups you join.

There Are Special Dress Requirements for Membership in a Group

> There is a gathering at which requirements in wearing apparel are being discussed. Evidently I am in a group, or want to belong to a group, that has announced special requirements in "dress." They are being very specific about the kind of material of which even undergarments are to be made. We are looking at a taffeta type underslip that is made of a high priced material. I feel this is too expensive. I have found something slightly different I think may meet requirements, but it is still expensive. Someone there with me is saying she thinks that is still a lot to be expected to spend. I agree, but I think I want to meet requirements somehow.

Did I want to conform in order to belong to some group? What did this entail? Even the material for the undergarments was being specified. Underwear can be a symbol for personal attitudes, intimate feelings, basic and underlying beliefs. Expensive clothing might indicate a desire to show off or depict an exaggerated sense of self-worth.

In the dream, others and I thought the cost to meet requirements would be too much. What was going on in my life that this might be referring to? What "group" might the dream be referring to? Costs might not be just "material" costs; there might be other kinds. Did the group require conformity in non-material ways? Did it want to set standards I must obey, tell me what to believe and feel about things and how to spend my time? The desire to belong is a powerful force. But I should carefully consider the cost. Did/do I feel comfortable, in agreement with the beliefs of the group? It sounds as if I had doubts since I stated I felt the cost was too much. Yet I wanted to find a way to make it possible.

Nine months later I had the following dream:

I Try On the Dress I'm Making; It Fits and I Like It

> I don't remember now where it takes place. I may be waiting for others to meet me. While doing so, I'm sewing a dress for myself. It is long and has a graceful flowing line. After sewing the side seams I try it on to see if it fits. I find that it does and I like it. I take it off so I can work on the finishing details.

In this dream I was making a new dress for myself. This might be a metaphor for changing my attitudes, seeing things in a different way, creating a new image for myself. Part way through the process I tried the dress on to see if it fit. I found that it did and I liked it. So I continued to work on the finishing details. I knew by this time that dreamwork was my passion and I was continuing in-depth studies.

This series was taking place during the same time I was struggling with another issue, which involved my spiritual life. I describe this in Chapter 22. It is interesting to note that the last dream mentioned above occurred about five months after I joined a more liberal church. Apparently a positive shift in how I look at myself and how I want to present myself to others was occurring on several levels. I was no longer trying to make myself conform to other people's ideas. I am deciding things for myself, creating my own image, with which I am pleased. I believe it fits me.

There is still another level on which this transformation was taking place. It was referred to in a dream that came near the beginning of this series. It had to do with my relationship to my parents—in particular in this dream to my mother.

I Don't Like Mother's Dress; I Have On No Clothes

I seem to be with several women preparing to go to
some gathering. One woman, maybe my mother, comes
in modeling a new dress she has gotten for this occasion.
She thinks the dress is very nice and correct for the
occasion and wants to know what we think. I refrain
from commenting because I don't especially like it,
although there is nothing particularly wrong with it.

Later at the gathering I want to leave before it is over.
I want to slip away. Some woman evidently gets me
to stay, but then at the end she is showing me the way
to leave without being noticed. At this time I realize
I'm not wearing any clothes—but no one seems to
notice—or at least no one says anything to me.

The dress my mother modeled might represent her ideas and attitudes towards what is proper to wear to gatherings, how to present oneself to others and in general her outlook on life. The dream indicated that I thought there was "nothing particularly wrong" with this, but evidently I might have different ideas. I probably didn't feel it was what I'd want to wear; I'd feel better in something different. Note that I said nothing to her to counter her approach; I didn't want to hurt her feelings or make a big issue of the situation.

The "shocker" seems to be that as I was leaving the gathering I discovered I had no clothes on. Nudity can represent baring yourself, revealing all, not hiding anything about yourself or trying to "put on airs" or create some special image.

"Mother," in the dream, can represent the "mother figure" within my psyche—in this case, that part of me that wanted to dress in a manner I thought appropriate for presenting myself to others. The incident doesn't represent a rejection of my mother; it represents a maturing relationship in which there's no longer a pulling or tugging at the "mother presence" within me. Now I am my own person. I'm free of any need to conform to expectations of my mother, to the images of myself that she projected onto me.

I wanted to leave the gathering early. Perhaps I didn't feel completely at ease at this particular event, but I allowed someone (some aspect of myself) to persuade me to stay. But as I was leaving, I became aware of my nudity. Even if other people had noticed this, they said nothing to me; i.e. if parts of my psyche were conscious of the fact I was showing my total self to the world, "they" didn't feel the need to say anything or to get me to cover up—put on a different persona. I was comfortable in and with myself.

—10—

Food in Dreams

Food nourishes our body. In order to grow and develop into healthy, mature human beings we need to take in the proper nourishment—the correct amount for our age and size and a balanced diet providing the needed nutrients. If we eat too much of the wrong kinds of food we might become overweight or we might bring on some ailment due to an imbalance of nutrients. If we do not get enough of the needed foods, our growth and development may be stunted.

Food for Thought

Food, in dreams, can represent whatever you take in, consume, to help you survive and grow mentally, physically, and spiritually. On the literal level we associate this with actual food that we eat. But it can also be food for thought—new ideas, new teachings, new beliefs, anything you take in and digest, intellectual or spiritual food for growth as an individual. Dreams always give the dreamer food for thought no matter what the actual subject. But then, sometimes, the subject is food.

If you need to prepare a special meal you might dream about possible items for the menu. Or you might dream the guests obviously don't like the special meal you prepared. The first dream would be an example of your unconscious bringing to consciousness material you probably had stored away and may have forgotten. The second one would be an anxiety dream showing you were worried about the upcoming event. These dreams can have metaphorical meanings in addition to the obvious ones. Their meanings would depend on your associations with all the images, the circumstances of the particular dream, and the feelings exhibited, both in the dream and lingering in the your mind after waking up (if these are remembered). Let's consider the following dream:

I Give Two Ladies the Food I Fixed for Myself or Someone Else

> I am planning to fix some food for two unidentified old ladies. First I fix some for myself or someone other than these ladies and am carrying it outside, up the street near a park. In recall, I'm not sure why. The two ladies appear in a car coming towards me. I debate in my mind whether to give this food to them or to make them wait 'till I have fixed something different as I originally planned. I decide I might as well give them this since they are here now. I return to my residence needing to fix something else for myself.

In the dream I had been planning to give two old ladies some food, wanting to be kind and helpful to people I figured might be needy. I ended up giving them the food I had prepared for someone other than these ladies, perhaps for myself. This was a dream in which I was putting other people's needs for nourishment ahead of my own. Although this might be considered admirable, it could be that I was blind to the fact that I need to take care of my own needs, to nurture myself. By looking after my own needs first, I can be better able to do for others. This uses the same principle that says, in an emergency situation on an airplane, put on your own oxygen mask before trying to help someone else.

In the following dream:

I'm Pulling Possibly Spoiled Food Out of a Freezer

> I'm investigating the contents of some large "chest" or similar object. It seems to be a freezer of some kind. I pull out things to see if they should be thrown away. Things have been in the container for a long time, and I'm suspicious—doubting that they could be safe to

consume. Some fat young man comes along. He may be
hungry and wants something to eat. He's hoping there is
something among what's in the container he can have. I
try to discourage this, saying things wouldn't be safe.

If in waking life I had learned that electricity had been off during an
absence, perhaps I was being reminded by my dreammaker to check out the
contents of my freezer. The dream would be warning about health in regard
to what is eaten. But the dream might be referring to food for thought.
The contents of the freezer had been there for a long time—perhaps an
image for outdated ideas that are no longer viable. Thus I should question
what thoughts and beliefs I have that I should get rid of, that are no longer
"safe to consume."

In another dream, *I'm Brought Uncooked Eggs for Breakfast*, I was
served inadequately cooked eggs. My father, who joined me for the meal,
was also served not-fully-cooked eggs. He insisted they be cooked properly
and sent them back. The "father figure" might represent the more assertive,
authoritarian part of myself (perhaps not fully conscious in me) that can
help me stand up for my rights. He might also be representing the parent
within who is seeing to it that only fully prepared, properly thought out
ideas were digested or experienced.

In the following dream, was I being discerning and wise or was I just
being stubborn?

I Refuse to Eat Some Food the Waitress Offers

I'm with Owen at a restaurant where we are well known.
The waitress is aware of our likes and dislikes. On this
occasion she comes to serve us some particular food
from a serving dish. She announces that she knows I
don't like such-and-such that is in this dish, but she
suggests I take a spoonful from the lower part that will
have just a little of the item in question. I consider it and
am about to accept the spoonful which I decide to refuse
it all together.

The food might represent some beliefs or ideas that I did not want to incorporate into my thinking. I evidently considered the possibility of accepting at least a little of whatever the particular substance represented, but then decided not to be pushed into going against what seemed right to me. On the other hand, the food referred to in this dream might be some actual food I needed to be consuming and I was being stubborn when I refused to try it. In this case my dreammaker might be trying to suggest I might benefit from it and I should give it a try. What did this represent in my waking life and could it possibly help me?

One more dream we will consider is this:

I Plan to Read and "Eat" a Newspaper

> I intend to be entertained by reading and "eating" a
> newspaper I have. I start to do so. After one taste of the
> paper I spit it out. It tastes awful; the quality of paper
> is bad. I won't continue to eat the paper. Do I want to
> ingest someone's written words?

This is certainly an interesting twist. Just consider all the circumstances, ideas, beliefs we find in newspapers. Imagine having to take into oneself the violence, tragedy, deception, grief, and sadness found in the news. I can understand why I would want to spit it out. Perhaps the dreammaker was trying to tell me I had been absorbing too much of the news, letting it "get to me." It is neither pleasant nor healthy to do so. Dreams come to bring to consciousness matters that really matter, so I should pay attention to this message.

Preparing Food for Others

I have had many dreams through the years in which I was preparing food for others. Since I don't do much cooking in waking life, the dreams evidently were speaking metaphorically about how I was working with ideas, integrating them into my own thinking, and preparing them for the intellectual nourishment of other people. Some years ago I had this dream:

I'm Preparing Food for a Group; The Stew's Not Working

> I am trying to prepare food that will be served at a large
> gathering. I don't have a fixed recipe to follow, but am
> experimenting with ingredients. At some point, when the
> stew is only partially done, I ask some other member of
> the group to see what I'm doing. The dark, almost black
> mixture probably doesn't have much taste, but I point
> out that I haven't added the meat yet. That will be what
> adds the most flavor. The other woman is dubious as to
> whether this is "working" and, also, is concerned that it
> isn't time yet for the occasion, which is some weeks off
> yet. She thinks I'm preparing it much too far in advance.
> I say I'm simply experimenting now, practicing. . . .

A stew is made up of a mixture of ingredients, a combination of several
ideas, which would create the end product that would be served the group.
I was not following a fixed recipe; I was experimenting. Meat, still to be
included, represented the most important part. In fact, I stated it "will be
what adds the most flavor."

I assume the dream referred to some project or presentation I was
working on. I appeared to be working carefully through my thoughts
and ideas well in advance of the time I was due to make a presentation.
However, I had more work to do before it is ready for consumption.

Let's consider this dream further. I might ask myself if I really intended
to put actual meat in a stew or was I using the term only metaphorically
as the main ingredient in my thinking, which had not yet fallen into
place, into the cooking pot. I also note a reference to the mixture being
"dark, almost black." This makes me think of black beans. Beans can
be a diet "staple"; they can be just as basic as meat. Had I already put
these in the pot, but didn't want to reveal this? The other woman, some
aspect of myself, doubted whether the mixture was "working." Black beans
are considered to be very nutritious, a basic part of a healthy vegetarian
diet. Whatever they represented in my thinking will be very nourishing;
therefore I should not hesitate to include them in my recipe, in the mix of
ideas in the presentation for which I was preparing.

Six months earlier, I had dreamed about another meat stew. This dream had a very different message.

A Woman Asks for Alternative Food; Says a Law Requires It Be Available

> I am with several people at mealtime. The "meal" is
> being served out of a bowl placed on a pedestal up
> on a platform. I believe it is a meat-based stew. I hold
> up my bowl to receive it as someone dips it out, but
> I am wishing I could have something different since
> I shouldn't have beef. But I assume this is all that is
> available and I will have to eat it. A female who comes
> along behind me asks for something different, calling
> forth some special law which evidently states the right to
> have some alternative food. The server seems reluctant
> and suggests something already available, although there
> is nothing else visible. The woman asks for something
> specially cooked. She points out that the law makes this
> possible. Although the server doesn't like the idea, he
> finally agrees to fix what the person asks for.

The dream might be indicating a wish to be vegetarian or my inner dreammaker's recommendation that I should be. On the collective level, the dream could also be pointing out women's desire to be allowed alternative ideas and beliefs. I take note that the serving bowl had been put up on a pedestal, a special place of honor. I wonder who put it there. Since meat is considered the staple food for the majority of people and often is called "a real man's dish," the dream might be referring to the feeding of ideas and beliefs put forth in our patriarchal society. Women in recent years have gained rights formerly withheld from them. Might this be "the law" the woman refers to?

Since all people in a dream represent aspects of the dreamer, the unidentified woman represented a part of me that had become aware of the new rights that should be allowed me, while the "I" in the dream, the ego, still felt I would have to accept what is offered even though I would prefer something different.

Dreams of food can provide us with a wide variety of information about our life situations and ourselves. It is important to pay attention to:

- which food is indicated
- who prepares it
- where it is eaten and by whom
- the consumer's reaction to the food or to the person doing the cooking.

This sounds as if we are discussing any ordinary encounter with food in our everyday life. However, dreams can be metaphorical, informing us on many levels—mental, physical, emotional, or spiritual.

Being Deprived of Food

Over a seven-year span from August 1997 to August 2004 I had a series of dreams in which I felt deprived of food. It began with this one:

I'm Being Deprived of Food

I am with several other people—don't remember who.
We are in a situation where food is being served. I am
not being allowed to have any. I believe someone is
deliberately keeping me from getting any. I feel deprived.

At the time of this dream I needed to avoid certain foods because of food sensitivities. I was frustrated when eating out at special occasions when my particular dietary needs could not be accommodated and I feared I'd not get enough to eat. So this was the literal level the dream probably was addressing. Two months later someone tried to take my food away before I finished eating in this dream:

Don't Take My Food Away

I'm eating in a restaurant or cafe. I'm about to finish my
meal when two workers try to clear away the dishes. I

reach for my plate to keep the food. They are alarmed
when I say "No" and reach for the remaining food. . . .

In another dream six months later, while visiting my family I left the
dinner table to do something before I had finished eating.

I Mustn't Show I'm Upset that My Remaining Food Was Taken Away

. . . I return and find that my plate has been taken
away. They assumed I was through. I explain that I had
intended to eat the jello carrot salad that had been on
the plate. I feel upset, but must say it's okay.

Unfortunately, although I had been deprived, I felt I must be polite and
uncomplaining, even though all my needs were not being met.

A year later I had a dream in which *I'm Upset Because the Waitress
Takes Away Some of My Food*. She "announces I can't have that much and
spoons some fruit from my plate. . . . I am protesting while she does this,
saying no one was there to serve me so I took some. . . ." Bravo! I was finally
speaking up for myself.

Then, still three more years later, in a dream

A Friend Invites Me to Eat with Her at the Restaurant Even Though It's Closed

I'm at a restaurant, visiting someone who works there. It
evidently is a day when the restaurant is not open to the
public. When lunchtime comes, she invites me to have
some lunch with her there. I question whether it's okay.
She assures me it is. Later some other people appear at
the door wanting to find food. They are told the place in
closed.

The woman in the restaurant symbolized a part of me that wanted to give
myself nurturing. The ego, the "I" in the dream, questioned this and was

not sure it was okay since the public was excluded. This dream suggested I needed to pay more attention to my own needs, less to the public's.

Then about a year and a half later, in a dream

The Food on the Table Is Not for Me

> In an unidentified location, maybe someone's home
> or a restaurant, I come up to a table where a female
> acquaintance is seated, eating from a wide selection of
> food at her place. I assume I am to eat with her, so I sit
> down at the table. I also assume I'm to share the food
> that's on the table. Somehow I learn this food is just for
> her and nothing has been brought for me.

Gillian Holloway, in *The Complete Dream Book*, explains this type of dream: "Food typically represents a kind of experience or a type of energy to be taken in. One such dream is that of being at a banquet yet being unable to eat due to some restriction. This suggests that the rich experiences of life are somehow being held at bay by an inner restriction or due to circumstances beyond your control."

This was a long series dealing with restrictions about food. I needed to figure out what restrictions in my life made me feel deprived. Perhaps I was not nourishing/nurturing myself enough. I might still have been frustrated over diet restrictions due to food sensitivities. Or, were there restrictions in some other areas of my life? Perhaps further dream explorations will provide some answers.

—11—

COLOR AND MUSIC IN DREAMS

According to dream researcher Robert Hoss, our association to color in our dreams can show us "the emotional conditions that stimulated a dream or dream image." As Hoss reports in his book *Dream Language,* extensive research showed that "for the most part color comes from a normal brain function that associates emotion with sensory input" and "that color imagery in dreams contains emotional content that relates in some way to the content within the dream image and the emotional situation in the dreamer's life."

He also states: "Sometimes . . . the dreamer's associations with the color can reveal hidden feelings or reactions to the emotional memories within the dream image. The color essentially 'paints' the image with the dreamer's emotional response to it."

As a result of his research into how color experienced in dreams corresponds to specific emotional events experienced by the subjects around the time of the dreams, Hoss has devised a questionnaire with "statements . . . designed to trigger your own personal associations with a situation the dream might be dealing with." These statements "do not represent the 'meaning' of a dream color and should not be used as a dictionary of color meaning. . . . The statements are also designed to provide a spectrum of emotions, from being 'filled with the emotion,' to needing more of that emotional stimulus. Your own particular situation would naturally be limited to just a few statements." If none of the statements triggers an association, then you can freely associate with your own feelings about the color.

Hoss also devised a role-play technique he calls *image activation dreamwork* that quickly reveals "the emotional content and possible conflicts within a dream image and relates them to the dreamer's waking life situation." The dreamer is asked to imagine he "becomes" a dream image or character that seems important, curious, or impacting, preferably such an image in color. As this image or character, the dreamer completes statements describing who he is, his purpose or function, likes and dislikes, and fears and desires.

The results of this process can be compared to the dreamer's choice of statements that contain emotional themes reportedly associated with the color or colors in the dream. The dreamer is to choose the statement/s "that really stands out, that provides the greatest 'aha' or connection with your waking life situation." Hoss believes that if "the color of an image and the image itself emerge in the dream from the same emotional stimulation, their associations should be similar."

Using the above techniques, let's see what we can learn about the following dream Owen had years ago:

Violent Garage Confrontation

I am in what appears to be a garage with space for perhaps two cars. I have been unexpectedly confronted threateningly by a man who seems strong, angry, and menacing. He overpowers me and presses me hard against the back wall in a rectangular box, with cutouts for my neck, arms, and lower legs. I struggle forcefully and begin to break free, temporarily pushing my assailant to the floor. There is a dark blue or black SUV-type vehicle parked in the space beside us, with an open sunroof. I break fully free and jump and clamber on top of the car and start feet first down into it through the opening of the sunroof. My assailant is up and rushing to try to catch and stop me. I wake up before the outcome is clear, but the impression seems to be that I am escaping harm.

Imagining himself as the SUV-type vehicle, Owen responded that he was "powerful, unafraid, menacing though not necessarily in an evil sense, and is to be taken seriously." His purpose was "to provide secure and safe transportation." He liked "the power, authority, trustworthiness, strength, and sense of control." He disliked "his inflexibility, limited utility, and not being a fun car." What he feared most was "loss of control and rollover on the highway." What he desired most was "to break out of the mold and run free and see the world."

I next asked him if the dream image of being up against the wall corresponded to any feelings he had in waking life. He responded that he felt "boxed in by oppressive life circumstances and obligations, by certain traditional and inflexible spiritual views, and by certain professional and spiritual elements in my professional and personal life that might prove to be inadequate when confronted with potential difficulties that may lie ahead." He felt "the need to break free of certain limiting, constricting beliefs, and to reframe aspects of my world view and spiritual perceptions/views."

He saw the SUV as a means of escape from "the circumstances around me that put me in the box, but at the same time I am still in a self-made and self-perpetuating box." This led him to the realization that "I'm not simply the victim of the circumstances and context that boxed me in, I have boxed myself in."

Next I read the statements Hoss lists for the color blue, followed by the color black. After hearing the list of seven statements for the color blue, Owen said he resonated slightly with the following three: "I need rest, peace or a chance to recuperate. I need a relationship free from contention where I can trust and be trusted. I need a peaceful state of harmony offering contentment and a sense of belonging."

Statements attributed to the color black resonated more strongly. He thought the dream itself showed that "I am fearful of or intimidated by the situation" and "I have been dealt an unacceptable blow." Then the following three seemed to state his personal emotions most strongly: "I refuse to allow it/them to influence my point of view. I can't accept the situation and don't wish to be convinced otherwise. I feel the need for extreme action, perhaps in revolt against or to compensate for the situation."

When black and blue are paired in a dream, Hoss' list combines these emotional themes this way: "I have an urgent need for peace and a chance to rest. I need to be lovingly understood. I feel I am treated with a lack of consideration. I want others to comply with my requests."

When we began the discussion of his dream, Owen felt the dream was insignificant and not important enough to merit study. When we concluded, he was amazed by what it revealed and how close the emotional themes suggested by color and the metaphorical dream images matched his waking-life situations and feelings.

The important next step for Owen was to figure out ways to *honor* the dream, respecting his own needs and desire "to break out of the mold and run free and see the world," ways he could best put to use the insights he had gained through the exploration of this dream.

Hoss' statements cover a range of emotions from one end of the spectrum to its opposite. The statements that connect, along with the dreamer's associations with each dream element, can help construct a new understanding of the dream through which the dreamer can learn more about himself or herself. Also, the dreamer can consider his/her own associations to the color and how they affect his/her understanding of its use in the dream. In addition, a person's cultural associations to the color may be unique and will be significant. You can find the listing of "emotional associations" for each basic color in Hoss' book, *Dream Language.*

Music in Dreams

Music can affect us emotionally in many different ways. Lyrical, classical music can bring tears of joy to men's eyes. Music can soothe us, create feelings of inner harmony, and lift our spirits. Music can also help alleviate various physical problems and enhance communication.

However, certain types of music can accentuate our anxieties, trigger our fears, and set our nerves on edge. How it affects us depends not only on the basic rhythms and sounds involved but also our own past experiences and associations with the particular kind of music. These elements will also influence our understanding of the music's significance in our dreams. We need to take note of the context within the dream and what is going on in our waking life at the time of the dream.

Let's consider a brief dream:

While Riding in My Car a Man Sings a Beautiful Song with Me

> I'm riding somewhere with a man. I'm singing a
> soft, melodic song with him. It sounds beautiful. He
> is pleased with it too, says it will be a great success
> (evidently we are to perform somewhere together).

If I was preparing to perform with the man in waking life, this might simply be a dream rehearsal for an upcoming event. However, this was not the case.

A man in a woman's dream can represent her unconscious psychological masculine attributes—a potential for being hard, assertive, logical, and dominating. Feminine characteristics include being soft, receptive, giving, empathic, and nourishing. We need to have an appropriate proportion of both masculine and feminine aspects to be a "whole" person.

I was pleased to learn that my masculine and feminine aspects were expressing themselves harmoniously. It was suggesting that future endeavors, in which I will be aided by positive masculine attributes, are likely to be successful.

Four years later, I dreamed:

I Enjoy Singing While Dressing; I Announce I'm Pregnant

> I'm on the second level of a large building, getting
> dressed to go to a special occasion. After searching
> through my available clothes for something that will fit
> and will be appropriate to the occasion, I get dressed in
> an elegant long dress of a satin material.
>
> While getting ready, I begin singing to myself a very
> melodic song. My voice comes out strong and clear and
> I enjoy singing. I walk by the window and see there are
> a couple of people on the ground below who hear my
> singing. I continue singing and they give signs that they
> are enjoying what they hear.

had the distinct advantage of being conscious and remaining an active participant in the self discovery process."

At a Group Dreamwork Training Institute weekend I attended years ago three therapists trained in GIM gave an overview of how the process works. A specially trained therapist, using appropriate music, skillfully guides the client through the experience, which encourages unresolved issues to surface. As he relaxes into the music, the client allows any images that come to lead where he needs to go.

Carol Bush states: "Since people image in their own style the experience need not be all visual. There are kinesthetic imagers who are more aware of bodily sensations. Conceptual imagers make contact with an associative flow of ideas, and intuitive imagers have an intuitive sense of knowing though the imagery may be sparse. As you remain focused on your immediate experience, allowing it to 'speak' in its own language, you need only stay with the spontaneity of the experience."

This work energizes the psyche to heal itself. It can help to remove mental, emotional, and spiritual blocks, and can awaken new levels of creativity. Through this process, one may experience emotional releases, new insights, and often a spiritual unfolding.

One of the trainers, who is a clinical psychologist, told how she herself had a very transformative experience by bringing a dream image to this form of therapy. In her dream she was showering in a motel. She recounted:

A Therapist's Dream

I emerge from the shower and see something moving under a pile of clothes and debris. I realize that I had forgotten about my dog and that she is under the clothes and debris. I see that the lower parts of her front legs have been hacked off or chewed off or somehow dismembered from her body. I see her legs, these little bloody stumps, thrown in a corner. I panic and pick her up and rush her out of the room. . . . I have such deep feelings of anxiety and guilt . . . .

In the dream, fearing her dog might die she tried to call 911, but the phones wouldn't work. She rushed out of the motel. A woman and an ambulance approached, whisked the dog away to an emergency vet, but did not allow her to come along. She was left "standing there worried and without any way to get in contact with them." She tried to call several vet offices, but again, the phones did not work. When she saw a friend walking up the street with white flowers in a flower pot, she was very puzzled, wondering "if the flowers are flowers of condolence (the dog is dead) or . . . 'get well soon' flowers." She woke up from the dream very distressed and disoriented.

She took the dream images of the dog and its hacked off legs as well as the overwhelming feelings of fear and anxiety into two GIM sessions. Her intention was to explore the dream image in greater detail and to understand the strong emotion that accompanied it. She told us that she had an amazing experience and insight into her dream images and feelings.

Since people, animals, and other images in dreams can represent aspects of the dreamer, the therapist's dog could be a symbol for an aspect of herself.

"What resulted from the first GIM session," she explained, "was a deep and profound understanding of the sadness about my own legs being battered and bloodied from all the work they have done during the first half of my life. I was left with the need to honor these legs and just feel the depth of my feelings of gratitude and love for 'these bloody little stumps.'"

The reference to legs here is not to be taken literally, but metaphorically. In waking life, legs provide physical support; metaphorically, they might provide emotional or conceptual support.

"The second GIM session resulted in an awareness that I could honor these 'stumps' while 'growing new legs for the second half of my life.' I was informed in this session that the second half of my life would not be as difficult as the first half. I had an image and kinesthetic feeling that my new legs were being filled with gold and that they were tattooed with beautiful tribal bands. I had a deep sense and knowing that the 'beautiful and primitive strength would be with me always.' It was an amazing experience and one that has changed my life. I indeed feel that I have new and strong legs to stand on!"

Carol Bush explains further: "Music induced imagery seems more accessible to conscious association than the more hidden content of dream imagery. Yet in GIM it is not only the symbolic significance of the images that emerge but also the releasing potential of the imagery that contributes to the healing experience."

GIM is best suited for persons with depression, anxiety and most stress-related and relationship problems. It is helpful for those who find themselves in life transitions, such as career change, geographical moves and divorce. It is very well suited to persons with addictions, especially those who are in recovery. "GIM is not recommended for serious mental disorders."

—12—

FEARS REVEALED IN DREAMS

Dreams often bring into consciousness one's deepest fears. These fears may have been festering in the unconscious for some time. When we are ready to deal with them, when our "inner knowing" decides it is time for us to be conscious of these fears so we can do something about them, they may appear in our dreams. But as we know, they may be shown to us metaphorically as well as literally.

Fears at Retirement

As one approaches retirement from lifelong work, one might well have many fears about what the future may hold. When my husband was approaching retirement, he had a series of dreams all the same night which showed some of his anxieties about the future. The first was this dream:

Major Change for Historic Building

> I am walking around the campus where I work.
> Everything is in chaos. One building is "roped off" in
> preparation to be torn down or renovated. It is at the
> center of the campus. Everyone goes there after they
> leave their own building . . . . This building has been
> many different things over the course of its life—house,
> dorm, gym, post office, campus cafe, etc.

While discussing this dream I asked him for his associations with aspects of this dream. He replied, "The campus has been my life. The central building has been many things. Now it is being prepared for renovation. My role is being prepared for change."

Another dream of the series was:

Crash Test Turns Catastrophic

> The college is doing a crash test program with cars and
> dummies. The scene becomes the town hall building
> in the town where I grew up. We live in an apartment
> at the top of the building. The crash test is being
> conducted in the basement. I am attending a committee
> meeting nearby. I turn, see the crash, and the building
> begins to crumble. My wife is in the apartment on the
> top floor. I turn to the others screaming, at least twice,
> "Rachel is there in the apartment."

When asked about his associations for this part he replied, "The crash test represents the possible impact of sudden change. The building represents my childhood, my life, my father (whose office was on the top floor) and his influence upon my life. My wife, the most important thing to me, is included in this fragmentation and collapse of everything in my life."

A third dream in the series was the following:

I Fear My Wife May Leave Me

> My wife and I are having a very serious discussion in
> which I tell her I fear she is going to leave me to do
> something else with her life (not for another man). I
> seem to feel it is a choice between me and this other
> thing. Both are not possible.

This dream expressed Owen's same fear of losing me that he felt in the other dream. If these were my dreams, they would help me realize just how much I was worrying about my future. I certainly had the feeling that everything seemed to be coming apart.

In the dream about the crash test program there were several additional symbols and/or metaphors to be considered. Both cars and building are often symbols for ourselves and/or how we get around in our life. Being "in the basement" might refer to being in our unconscious. The apartment on the top floor might refer to our mental activities. So if this were my dream and I have been a very cerebral person, it might be showing my unconscious fear that my way of life was being tested. I also associate what was the apartment where my wife and I lived in the dream with the office space where my father worked when I was a young adult. I was horrified when I saw the building crumble. I feared I would lose everything, including my wife. The second dream in this series even said this literally. In addition I had been worrying about what I thought she wanted to do with her own life. I feared she must make a choice, one of which couldn't include me.

Spouses might find it difficult to share fears with one another. I am grateful that Owen is willing to share his dreams with me. This provides one way I can learn of his concerns and fears and then be able to reassure him that these have been needless worries. Fears often blow concerns greatly out of proportion. Calm and thoughtful discussions can bring understanding to all parties. As I have stated elsewhere this is possible *if both* people in a marriage or any other relationship understand the language of dreams and how to explore them. From his many years of experience of facilitating dream work with groups and individuals, Jeremy Taylor has seen and assures us that "dream sharing helps change the way we relate with others face to face. Everyone dreams, so this is a very good way to work with anyone and to make connections with him or her."

Captivity and Freedom

The following discussion is of an entirely different type of fear. Have you ever dreamed that you were being held captive and were trying to escape? Such a dream would be easy to understand if you were actually in prison, or a holocaust survivor, or a prisoner-of-war. But why would an ordinary person living in a peaceful society have such a dream?

In my late 30s I dreamed:

I Fear Being Attacked by Wild Boars, Wolves, Birds, and Humans

> Our family is imprisoned in a strange tower home
> surrounded by a fence and near an ocean. At first we
> are allowed outside for periods of time, but we always
> have to come back in. At times we have to hurry in to
> escape pursuit by fierce animals such as wild boars and
> wolves. We know we are being plotted against by an
> enemy, humans who control the wild beasts, too. We
> feel it is just a matter of time before things will go from
> bad to worse. On one occasion whole flocks of birds
> (perhaps gulls) are out in front near the ocean and they
> stalk nearer and nearer the house or tower devouring
> something off the ground. At times we have to climb the
> fence to get in to safety before being caught.

Confinement in dreams can represent a set of beliefs or patterns of behavior that inhibit one's personal development. These may have been inherited from strict or authoritarian—or just fearful—parents. They could be beliefs imposed upon us by local community, cultural, or religious groups.

It seems to me there was a double trap in this dream. My family was imprisoned in a tower home, but I seemed more fearful of beasts and birds outside the enclosure or the humans who controlled them. My associations to the word "tower" will be helpful in understanding the dream and its message. At the time of the dream, I lived on a college campus and thought of the term "ivory tower" which is often applied to institutions of learning. Evidently I felt confined in such an environment. Yet when I was "allowed outside," I felt threatened by the beasts and the birds that were controlled by humans.

Dreams can have objective, subjective, and/or universal meanings. Perhaps there were problematic situations I was facing in my relationships both inside and outside my immediate community. But on the subjective level, all dream figures may represent aspects of my own psyche. What do the birds and animals represent in me and why I am afraid of them?

Have my inherited beliefs caused me to be fearful of what I find in the outside world? Why did I feel the situation would only get worse and what might I be able to do to make things better? I have been considering these questions periodically for four decades. Yes, I did inherit certain beliefs that made me fearful in various personal and social situations and caused me to overreact when I felt threatened. The statement "Things will go from bad to worse" is an example of my overreactions—a sign of immaturity at the time. Experiences and growing maturity made me aware that the threats were not real. Through reading, counseling, and dreamwork, I have gained insights that have enabled me to work through issues within myself and with other people. However, this did not happen all at once.

Twenty-three years later, in January 1995, I was still dreaming of being in prison. But at that time I was actively trying to escape. In the summarized version of this dream,

I'm Trying to Escape an Institution

I am a prisoner of some group and am trying to escape. I'm not in a cell or confined in that way, maybe just confined in a building or institution. I go up to someone seated at a table and ask if I can use some paper they have. I'm not sure if there is already something on the paper, maybe a painting. I act as if I want to draw or paint on it, so that my "captors," if they are watching, will not realize what I'm really doing. I want to write an appeal for help. I turn to a page deeper in a stack, or in a book, and write: "Please help me escape. I'm being held prisoner" or something kin to this. I'm not aware of any immediate response or help.

Later I'm still trying to figure out how to get away and out of the building. There is a last door to go out. I devise a method I think might work. I watch a woman who is leaving go to the exit area and she throws her keys—or something—over onto a counter at a place to the side near the entrance. This is evidently what is done

when you leave the building. I decide that maybe if I do
the same thing—acting very natural as I do this—no
one will suspect anything wrong and I'll be able to leave.
I do this—"the routine"—while the woman I appealed
to for help is there. Maybe she thought of this as a way
of showing me how I can escape. She watches "with a
knowing eye" and saying nothing as I toss the keys onto
the counter. I either wake up or the dream shifts at this
point.

George R. Slater suggests in *Bringing Dreams to Life* that "[i]mages of
public buildings, such as institutional, governmental or business buildings,
malls, and apartment buildings, inasmuch as they are impersonal, may
refer to being trapped in collective thinking, where the individual is
submerged by the institution. Inasmuch as they are manmade, they may
refer to structures of a person's own life experience that have been socially
imposed."

As I have matured, my psyche has been constantly working on
various issues. In 1995 Owen and I were making plans for building a
new home at Lake Monticello near Charlottesville as Owen's first step
towards retirement. He would commute three days a week back to the
college to teach for the final two years before full retirement. My psyche
likely interpreted this move as escaping an institution—but not complete
freedom. So six months after the above "escape" dream I dreamed:

I Make My Escape, But I Fear I'll Be Found and Made to Return

I want to escape from where I am. I find the
opportunity simply to walk off and out of where I'm
imprisoned while the "guards" are not watching. I
continue walking at a very rapid rate, wanting to get as
far away as possible as quickly as possible. I continue
for a long time—always with the feeling that I will be
found and made to return. I don't remember details, but
I think this is what happens.

We moved into our Lake Monticello house in June of 1996. Then in October I dreamed:

A Woman, Trying to Help Us Escape, Slips Me Some "Stone Currency"

> I'm being handed some stones or stone fragments, which
> are the currency of this country, by a woman from the
> country. [It was not spelled out initially in this dream,
> but I think I was in a foreign country.] She is slipping
> this to me "on the sly" as a way of trying to help me—or
> us—escape. I put them in my left pocket of the jacket
> I'm wearing. I later tell and show Owen what I was
> given.

This dream suggests that my inner feminine was attempting to help me leave a confining situation, to break away from constricting thoughts and beliefs. Our new physical location was providing at least a partial break from the actual and/or perceived confinements we had experienced at our previous residence, where we had lived for 30 years. But, apparently the move did not bring an immediate shift in my psyche concerning the feelings of confinement.

Owen's full retirement began in May of 1998. By this time I was participating in a Group Dreamwork Training Institute, learning all I could about dreamwork. At this time my dreammaker seemed to be describing this stage of my transition and transformation in the following dream.

I'm Being Held Captive and Unsuccessfully Try to Find a Way Out Through the Basement

> I'm in a large house. Many other people are there also.
> At some point I have the feeling that I am being held
> captive and I must escape. I decide to go down through
> the basement, believing I will find a way out there.
> Opening the door into a dark room I find several people

and make a hasty retreat, not wanting to disturb the
occupants and believing there is no way out that way.
Back up on the main floor I still try to find a way out.

Since I consider going into a basement going into one's unconscious, I
might think I didn't want to disturb (encounter) what I found there and
retreated, hoping for a different way out. But I suspect I really needed
to stay and make my way through the "dark room." As I have indicated
earlier, the journey toward consciousness is not easy. We must be willing to
explore previously unknown rooms in our psyche to learn what has trapped
us. Our psychological freedom is as important as, or even more important
than, actual physical freedom.

My psyche continued to work on this issue. In July 2001, this
dream:

Owen and I Are Confined Within an Institution

Owen and I are in some kind of "institution" which
my mind labels a "prison," but not one in which we are
behind bars. We have some "freedom" of movement
within the walls, but we can't leave. Much more
forgotten.

Then in May 2005 I'm still seeking release:

I Hope to Be Released from Prison

I seem to be in a prison, but I have hopes of being
released soon. . . .

I am not sure what triggered these last two dreams. The cause of feelings
of confinement may change through the years as a result of changed life
circumstances and a gradual shifting of beliefs.

In early 2008, my unconscious was still working on the matter of
beliefs, as shown in the following dream:

I'm Anxious to Find a Way Out of the "Castle/Amusement Center"

Owen and I are in a building that has the appearance
and "feel" of a castle sitting high up on a hill. We find
ourselves in a large area with many doors and many
people. We, along with others, are trying to find our
way out of this space. However, whenever we try to
open a door, it appears to be locked. Occasionally
someone seems to find a way out, but we can't figure
out how s/he does it. At some point Owen disappears
and I have no idea where he has gone. I begin to feel
desperate. I see a woman over to one side who I sense
may know "the secret" (to finding a way out of this
confinement). She seems to be just hanging around as if
she has some official role at this "amusement center." I
go over and almost beg for help, expressing my sense of
despair and desperation. The woman smiles knowingly,
but acknowledges she can't tell me; I must figure out
the solution for myself. She hints at something to do
with buttons, saying something simple and obvious.
(I don't recall what this is.) I go back to the doors and
finally spot something, perhaps the buttons that she
mentioned. I try pushing one and, sure enough, a door
opens to the outside. I hurry out, joining a crowd of
people heading down a path leading from this high
location. I can tell that at some distance down the
path it appears to get terribly steep. I think I see people
sliding swiftly down at that point. It looks dangerous,
but obviously it is the only way to go.

I associate the castle situated on a high location with an archetypal storybook
castle. I also think of the "ivory towers" that suggest to me institutions of
learning and connect this dream to the earlier ones discussed above.

In this new dream, Owen and I found ourselves with many others
in another confining place and we were trying to open the locked doors
that would provide a way out. As in an earlier dream, I ask a woman for

help. This time, although my inner feminine would like to help, she could only hint at the solution. We must make the effort to find the solution for ourselves. So here is one more metaphoric dream showing my desire to escape the confines of thoughts and beliefs that were hindering my development. Evidently I still needed to figure out which beliefs I needed to change.

I note, in reflection on this last dream, that I termed the confining space an "amusement center." We entertain ourselves constantly with our chattering thoughts. In the dream I "push the right button" and make it out to join others who have escaped. I needed to figure out what "the right button" represented in waking life. Perhaps the very steep and seemingly dangerous descent we still must go down represented going down into our unconscious. In the dream this was the only way to completely get away from the confinement in the "castle."

In a second dream the same night,

I'm Trying to Find My Way Home

> I am trying to find my way home from a meeting or conference. I have many "papers" with me as well as my pocketbook. I seem to be having trouble figuring out just where I am and which direction I should go. At some point where I have stopped, perhaps to rest/ sleep, I become alarmed when I realize my things have disappeared. I become frantic, fearing I won't be able to find my way home without the papers and my pocketbook that contains my money and my identification. I'll be stuck where I am. I'm relieved when someone helps me find/spot my pocketbook. At least I'll have means to continue on my way.

I equate "home" with our place of origin to which we return at the end of our earthly life. I was trying to find my way there after attending meetings and/or conferences (all the places I go to try to receive guidance for my journey through life), but I was not sure "where I am and which direction I should go." I feared the loss of my credentials and my money would prevent me from being able to continue on my way. I was relieved when someone helped me find what I thought was lost. This would seem to be a positive outcome; but is it? Perhaps I was too attached to my identification with my ego. Perhaps I still needed to learn to let go. David Gordon would classify this as a Dream of Attachment, as he discusses in his book *Mindful Dreaming*. He points out we need to let go of these kinds of attachments to allow something new to emerge in our life. Gordon, in an article about his book, states, "Dreams of Attachment and Letting Go prompt us to grieve and release our attachment to the causes of our suffering. In so doing we awaken—much like those who report near-death experiences—to a deeper contentment and fuller peace than we ever imagined."

David Richo in *The Five Things We Cannot Change: And the Happiness We Find by Embracing Them* presents many of the same ideas, perhaps in a slightly different manner. He states, "Paradoxically, an unconditional yes to who I am, how others are, and what the world is places me in the best position to grow. We can say yes to participating in our own evolution and working toward our life purpose in three ways: by cultivating psychological health, spiritual maturity, and mystical oneness or spiritual awakening. These are not three levels that follow one another linearly; they stand as one integral whole. Each is complete only when it includes the other two. To integrate these three dimensions of ourselves is to combine sanity and sanctity."

Dreamwork is one of the best ways we can "say yes to participating in our own evolution and working toward our life purpose." Dreams can help us understand what is going on within ourselves—emotionally, psychologically, spiritually, and physically.

My discussion has dealt with how these dreams are important to me personally. Personal dreams can also have a message for the collective. In the "castle" dream discussed above, my husband and I "find ourselves in a large area with many doors and many people. We, along with others, are trying to find our way out of this space." This suggests that an awakening may be taking place among many people—many who have been trapped as I have been by confining beliefs and are trying to find their way out.

The most recent prison/confinement dream that I have found while reviewing my dreams came in April 2012. Before I discuss it, let's see what has changed in my life during the last 15 years. Owen and I enjoyed living in the house I designed at Lake Monticello, with views of the water. Its location provided convenient access to the straightest highway to the college for Owen while he continued teaching. However, we disliked the increasingly dangerous, winding road into Charlottesville that we traveled for various reasons almost daily. So, after living at the lake for six years we built a beautiful home on the edge of Charlottesville. We came to love it, our neighbors, the convenience of its location, and the "offerings" of the town. We assumed we would live there the rest of our lives. But, advancing age and some health issues led us to rethink this idea after being there nine years. In the spring of 2011 Owen and I decided it was time for us to give serious consideration to moving to a retirement community. It had been in the back of our minds for years, but it was always something we might do eventually, but not yet. After visiting several places we agreed we liked one in the town where I grew up. All the logistics fell rapidly into place during the following summer and we made the move in October. We then experienced the physical and mental strains that naturally come after downsizing from the spacious home we owned into an apartment where we felt we were back in a college dormitory. Half a year after the move I had the following dream:

I Want to Escape Confinement

> I seem to be in captivity. My memory of any details has
> faded. I'm not in an actual prison, but I'm confined in
> some community. I'm "busy"—in my mind—trying to
> figure out how I can get away. I think I discover a way
> and as I'm about to leave I learn a male friend also wants
> to leave. I think I can help him (but I can't recall how).

The important phrase in this dream is "I'm confined in some community." I was not able to get out and about much for many months after the move due to a serious back problem that occurred just as we were making the decision to move. Thus I felt confined.

In the dream, "I'm 'busy'—in my mind—trying to figure out how I can get away" and "a male friend also wants to leave." I can relate this to the dialogue my husband and I have had with each other and in our individual minds. However, we are not actually thinking of leaving. We believe we made the correct decision. The ease with which the logistics of making the move fell into place led us to believe we were being guided by Spirit to make the move. But we miss our former location, friends, and familiar routines and places. One's ego doesn't like change and will search for a way to avoid it or to retreat back into the familiar. Our egos are really protesting the move; they want to go back to the familiar.

Dreams come to tell us something we are not aware of. We were already conscious of this struggle within our psyches, so what is this dream's message? I believe it is bringing into our consciousness the fact we will not be at peace with ourselves until our psyches accept this move. How can this be accomplished? What will it take to convince our recalcitrant egos to accept the move?

We are trying to be patient; we are trying to reconcile conflicting feelings. Major changes likely will involve some measure of compromise and real solutions are not necessarily perfect solutions. We can acknowledge our feelings, neither repressing them nor letting the issue define who we are. We can make a list of the reasons we decided to move and then create affirmations regarding the benefits, changing negative concerns and worries into the positive affirmations. An example might be: We worried about becoming unable to care for ourselves and/or each other as we age. The affirmation: We both will be cared for no matter what circumstances we might face. Although we regret giving up our life style and friends in Virginia, we have found the people in our new community to be very warm and friendly. We can welcome new friendships and opportunities for new endeavors. An example of how I used affirmations in the past: When faced with being treated with radiation for breast cancer, I was very fearful, but I was able to shift my consciousness away from fear. I went into a meditative state during each treatment and repeated various affirmations to myself and envisioned the radiation beams as healing energies vaporizing and eliminating any lingering cancer cells.

In addition, we can use methods used in working with nightmares to help bring a shift/transformation in our psyches. The suggestions in the above paragraph depend largely upon intellectual understanding of the opposing dynamics. However, a big part of our response to the situation is emotional. Thus, a different process might be more effective in shifting our feelings. This process is Guided Imagery for Dream Re-entry, used effectively by facilitators with patients in the International Association for the Study of Dreams Cancer Project. As Tallulah Lyons explains in *Dreams and Guided Imagery: Gifts for Transforming Illness and Crisis*, " . . . the dreamer re-enters the dream or nightmare with the intent to allow his or her relationship to the dream to transform. Guided imagery allows the dreamer to side-step rational thought and verbal interpretation. The process immerses the dreamer in a journey of emotional sensations and facilitates direct encounters with elements of the dream. This approach allows transformation at a sensate level. . . . Whatever you fear and resist will show up in dreams as a threat. When your fear and resistance begin to diminish, you will perceive the image and energy as less threatening, and in many situations life giving."

This process, also, requires our patience. It will take time, likely months, for a transformation to take place—time during which we can undertake additional re-entry sessions and meditative experiences, and perhaps journaling. During this time we can also record additional dreams, then notice any change in the situation or feelings towards the situation in question. This will give us some indication about the status of our psyche. We will very likely see a gradual shift, as we see illustrated in many of the dreams in this book. For fascinating examples and detailed instructions, along with suggested scripts to use with dreams and guided imagery, refer to Lyons' book *Dreams and Guided Imagery*.

Fears of Scarcity Revealed

In our modern Western culture there seems to be a predominance of fears, among them the fear of scarcity. In our private lives we approach life fearing we won't have enough of whatever we think we need. These fears are not only in our conscious awareness, but also show up in our dreams that come from our unconscious. In many dreams, which I discussed in Chapter 10 on Food in Dreams, I felt I was being deliberately deprived of food.

Then in another dream:

I Watch the Man Stuff Messy Food Inside His Coat

I'm seated across the table from an old man—not a
relative—at a meal. I watch as he takes some item of

food and puts it into his pocket. Nothing is said by him
or by me about this. There are other people at the table
with us. I'm not sure whether they notice his actions.
After a short time he picks up more food—covered with
a gooey, tomato-based sauce—and slips it inside his
coat. I notice the coat already has food stains. Evidently
he does this often. I think to suggest a better way to
take the food, but decide there's no point in doing so.
He gets up and leaves.

The old man represented a part of me that felt the need to horde food—
nourishment—for a later time, a part of me governed by a sense of scarcity.
Since the person was male, he is considered a masculine component within
me, with the characteristics our culture considers to be psychologically
masculine: aggressive in getting things done, logical, discriminating.
According to this dream he was also a part of me that fears scarcity. This
seems to be tapping into what Carl Jung called the *collective unconscious*,
the deepest layer of the human psyche that contains universal patterns and
forces—*archetypes* and instincts. To understand where the fear of scarcity
is coming from one should consider the following:

In Paleolithic and Neolithic cultures the divine feminine was supreme
in many locations throughout the world. As Adele Getty writes in *Goddess:
Mother of Living Nature*, the divine feminine was the "Mother of the
World, Giver of Life, the great nurturer, sustainer and healer." When the
early people left their caves in favor of settlements in the open fertile valleys
they lived peacefully without need of fortifications and weapons for over
a thousand years. Grain and game were abundant and free for the taking.
Later, partly as a result of cultivation of the land after the people gave up
a migratory, hunting and gathering existence, the ecological balance of an
area was upset and people experienced scarcity due to drought, famine,
flood, and blight. Along with this came the domestication of animals and
the realization of the male's role in conception. "The domination of animals
gradually resulted in the urge to 'domesticate' and subjugate women and
the Goddess," the divine feminine. Invading hordes also brought with them
weapons and violence. What had once been an atmosphere of pleasure and
abundance became one of fear, violence, and scarcity. This psychological

atmosphere from the collective unconscious is what is being tapped into in the above dream.

The dream suggests I needed to consider how to shift my thinking away from feelings of scarcity. Sometimes a suggested solution comes in another dream. In this case I actually had a dream with a possible solution six years before these other two dreams, but evidently its message hadn't registered with me. Let's see what it said.

I'm Pleased and Moved Emotionally by Gift from Craggy Old Woman

> As my husband and I leave somewhere, an older, large
> "craggy" woman, who is in a familiar grandmotherly
> role in the dream, jovially hands me an item that
> she takes from a pocket. I'm pleased and moved
> emotionally. I thank her, saying: "My grandmother used
> to do just that every time I left her."

I don't remember what I was given, but it evidently was something of significance, which pleased me and moved me emotionally. I remember my own grandmother as being a very warm, loving, kind, generous, and spiritually-centered woman. Thus I feel the "craggy" old woman represents the wise woman—loving grandmother—part of me that connects back to the divine feminine and all She represents. The dream was suggesting there are some elements of this life-giver, healer, and sustainer within me. Thus I need not fear scarcity.

Adele Getty also writes of "a North American Indian creation story which tells of a time long before any creature was born when all that existed was calmness . . . . This calmness was called the time-space void of Great Grandmother Wakan. Wakan is an ancient memory that all creation carries within itself . . . . Great Grandmother embodies the creative-receptive [feminine] energy of the universe." Mating with her masculine consort, Great Grandfather, or Skkuan, Great Grandmother conceives a freedom child called Wakan Tanka. "From this initial trinity the physical world is manifested."

I described the old woman as having "a familiar grandmotherly role." This could easily be the ancient memory we carry within us now appearing in the dream. She is the divine feminine who will tend to our needs. If we will let Her into our lives we can let go of thoughts of scarcity, greed and violence, we can return to the concept of sharing the bounty of the world with all its inhabitants. Individual dreams can have universal significance. If we will listen to and share such dreams, then take appropriate action, our world can become again one of beauty, joy, and abundance.

Death — Signs of Transformation

Dreams of death are often frightening to us. We may fear they are foretelling our own death or that of someone we know and love. Only rarely are such dreams precognitive. One of the most famous precognitive death dreams was one that Abraham Lincoln had, seeing himself laid out on a catafalque in the Capitol building. But this kind is extremely rare.

Most of the time dreams of death symbolize the death of some aspect of ourselves, such as outdated beliefs and undesirable attitudes, that we need to let go. This "death" will allow more "mature" aspects to come in, bringing us more into balance. We may be the persons dying, in the dream, or it might be someone else, actual or fictitious, who has the particular characteristic in question.

Owen had the following dream:

Life or Death Choice

> I have a choice to make about something. If I do the right thing it means I will die. I see my wife standing nearby with tears in her eyes and a smile on her face. I know I must make the choice in which I will die.

This dream occurred before Owen had learned how to understand the metaphorical nature of dreams. He had some serious obligations to fulfill during the next few days and he became very worried after having this dream. He feared the dream was saying he was about to die and he would not be able to meet these obligations.

If this was what the dream was saying, it would seem strange that I, in the dream, had a smile on my face along with tears in my eyes. I love my husband dearly and do not want anything bad to happen to him and he knows this. Why would his dreammaker have me reacting this way in the dream? Owen shared the dream with me and I reminded him that the dream could be referring to an aspect (characteristic or attitude) that it would be good to let go of. In other words, some part of him needed to die. It would be understandable for me to be smiling through my tears because I was pleased to know he was about to make a beneficial choice. After our discussion he was very relieved to realize he should not take the dream to be a literal recommendation. Needless to say he did not die and was fully able to meet his professional obligations. This illustrates how helpful it can be to know how to interpret your dreams. It can save you from needless worrying.

I know this from my own personal experience. I was alarmed by the following dream that came before I knew how to explore and understand dreams:

I Watch as My Father Is Killed by a Wedge

I enter a strange building that seems to be a cafe in a foreign place or some similar type establishment. As I walk in, in front of me I observe an archway and in the archway stands my father. As I watch, a wedge-shaped object from above my father's head falls down upon him hitting him on the very top of the head and he collapses to the floor. In my horror I scream three times: "My father's dead. My father's dead. My father's dead." And the dream ends.

Even though my father was in his nineties when I had this dream, the dream probably had nothing to do with the actual possibility that he could die in the next year or two. I was concerned about this dream and shared it with Dr. Vernon Sylvest, a medical doctor and counselor who understands dream symbology. At the time I knew nothing about dream symbols and metaphors. Sylvest pointed out that the dream is full of symbols. I could consider the figure of my father to represent a part of myself. As I have discussed in Chapter 5, I needed to let go of some of my attitudes and beliefs that had been set by my father's authoritarian views.

The cafe is a place for taking in food; food represents knowledge. The wedge-shaped object coming from above signified an event coming from a higher source. It hit the very top of the head, which is the area of the seventh chakra where the highest wisdom and enlightenment comes into the body, thus signifying a positive transformation was about to take place or was taking place.

As I look back now, I believe the dream was announcing the beginning of a special phase of my ongoing transformation. The timing of this dream fascinates me. It occurred early in 1990, which corresponds to the time I began my serious interest in and study of dreams. I would say that at that time I was beginning to take in much new "food for thought." During the two-plus decades since then, my metaphorical diet has been indeed rich. My dreams, coming from the Divine Source, have brought many amazing insights into my conscious awareness.

This dream occurred three and a half years before my experience with breast cancer. As I described in more details in my book *Guided by Dreams*, I consider the whole experience a life-transforming event. It was part of the larger picture of ongoing transformation.

The timing of the series of dreams in which I searched for my own glasses, discussed in Chapter 5, illustrates the fact that transformation is ever ongoing. They began eight years after this dream of my father's death and continued for six more years.

In these two "death" dreams above, circumstances indicated that the loss was a positive step. However, there could be times when a dream might symbolize an undesirable loss. We need to carefully consider all circumstances of the dream to see it they indicate we have neglected or misused a good quality or talent. Such a dream could also be a warning of a potential health problem resulting from poor health habits or abusive behavior and substances. A medical check-up might be a wise precaution.

If the dream is a warning or a suggestion for improvement, take appropriate steps. The dream might be showing you ways to help yourself. It might be announcing a transitional time in your life—a very positive experience, one that signifies growth in consciousness and changes in beliefs and attitudes.

We are usually alarmed and wary of change and transformation and the dying of the old part of ourselves. In the last dream above, I was horrified when my father collapsed and died. I was horrified at the thought of the loss. At the time I did not understand dream symbology; I was not aware of what a magnificent journey I was (and still am) experiencing.

Dreams of Approaching Death

When we are approaching actual death, the images in our dreams may symbolize in various ways the approaching transition. For an in-depth discussion of dreams of the dying I recommend *On Dreams & Death* by Marie-Louise von Franz, who worked closely with Carl Jung for 31 years and is now often acknowledged as Jung's intellectual heir. Von Franz discusses how dream symbols "psychically prepare the dreamers for impending death" and how "the unconscious psyche [the source of our dreams] pays very little attention to the abrupt end of bodily life and behaves as if the psychic life of the individual . . . will simply continue . . . . There are also dreams which symbolically indicate the end of bodily life and the explicit continuation of psychic life after death. The unconscious 'believes' quite obviously in a life after death." Obvious motifs that refer to approaching death include, among others, a clock that has stopped and cannot be started again or a tree that has been cut down and is lying on the ground. Von Franz connects numerous case studies of actual death dreams to themes of ancient and contemporary cultures and sheds new light on our assumptions about death, life, and a possible afterlife.

Dreams of the dying may reveal concerns and fears. Family members, friends, and health care workers can benefit from listening carefully. Maggie Callanan and Patricia Kelley in *Final Gifts* recommend asking the dying to interpret their own dreams instead of interpreting for them. They suggest we can help them identify their feelings, find solutions, and ease their passage through this important and natural transition in their life cycles.

Monique Sequin and Nicole Gratton in their book *Dreams and Death: The Benefits of Dreams Before, During and After Death* give a different suggestion. They recommend just asking, "Do you dream? Would you like to tell me your dream?" If the patient tells you a dream, just listen. You should not try to "dig" for any deep meaning. But you can share the dream with family members and health care professionals. The scenarios reveal the patient's stage of the dying process and how the patient is feeling about everything. They can help prepare the family to face the fact that their loved one is close to death and also help staff remember to deal with family dynamics. Sometimes a patient is keeping his feelings to himself, not wanting to burden family members. Dream sharing can open the door to communication, allowing the family to openly talk with the patient about what they will have to face eventually.

Even dreams of family members can be helpful. Sequin and Gratton tell of a dream of a daughter of a dying woman. The daughter had been concerned about the medications her mother was receiving—perhaps worrying about whether she was being given too much or too little. The daughter dreamed that her mother said she was okay and sleeping well, so the daughter relaxed and ceased worrying about the medication.

A dying man dreamed he was in a room with no windows or doors. When he told his wife, she suggested that when he saw a door he could just go on through it. Later he dreamed of a door, told his wife, and then died.

Sometimes the dying person hangs on, maybe feeling trapped, because he feels a spouse or family member still needs him or doesn't want him to die. In my version of this scenario, the wife's suggestion was a way to let him know it was okay for him to leave.

Patients can be comforted to know someone understands and they are not alone. Many families have felt a shared dream was a final gift to them and helped them in their bereavement process.

and worry about our families and friends. Somehow some of us survive, while others die. Either the water recedes or the snow melts and we begin looking for survivors. I don't find Marcia (our daughter) anywhere. I look and look and can't find her. I drive out into the countryside—into a valley searching for her. . . .

The dream ends or shifts before I find her. In 1998, I had this dream, which I have slightly abbreviated here:

We Prepare For, Then Survive, a Tidal Wave

I am in an institutional setting. We learn of a major natural disaster approaching. I feel we need to prepare to evacuate. We're told to gather a few things to take, including a warm coat. I try to decide what to take. I wonder about not having a pocketbook with identification and my birth certificate. I will just have to remember details of time and place of birth. I round up, in my mind, more than we would be able to carry. Word comes to be ready to leave. We see other young people from a neighboring building running by.

Next Owen is with us. He has gotten a report of where the trouble is and we're trying to see where it is on a map. We learn there is a major tidal wave approaching. It's now so close there is no point in trying to leave. We just need to find the safest place within our building. We look out a window and see the tidal wave approaching. We go to an inside wall where we take the framed pictures off the wall, then crouch awaiting the impact. It comes. We survive.

Afterwards we're seeking information on the damage in the territory around us. We hear awful sounds, the sounds of animals, terrified, wailing. We see off in the valley, beyond and below, terrified elephants, maybe zebras and other African animals—panicked—running.

. . . We also walk through the building to see who else
survived. We come upon a room full of babies and
young children . . . . We will help take care of them, but
I don't know how we'll provide.

What do these dreams mean? Were they warnings? Expressions of personal
concerns? Both? These dreams pointed to unconscious feelings of being
threatened. Upon reflection, I can now understand what was going on
at the time in my psyche. On a personal level, this 1998 dream about
an approaching tidal wave suggested that there was emotional turmoil
building in my life, possibly pertaining to my professional life since the
setting of the dream was an "institution," an established organization or
corporation of a public nature. I worried about not having my identification
with me. This might signify a fear that the conflict could shake my sense
of identity.

Animals in dreams often represent the instincts and habits we attribute
to them that are present in ourselves. After understanding what I felt the
threat was, I could figure out how these animals' attributes within myself
could help work through the problem.

It is often useful to seek additional information about the animals,
those we think we are familiar with as well as the more unusual and
exotic ones. I recommend three books by naturalist, mystic, and lecturer
Ted Andrews: *Animal-Speak: The Spiritual & Magical Powers of Creatures
Great & Small; Animal-Wise: The Spirit Language and Signs of Nature;*
and *Nature-Speak: Signs, Omens, and Messages in Nature.* In these books
Andrews gives us scientific, mystical, and mythological information about
the characteristics and qualities of plants and animals, drawing upon his
own naturalistic and mystical experiences and education.

Elephants are known for excellent memory, power, and intelligence
and for showing great affection and loyalty to each other. In *Animal-Speak,*
Andrews suggests those to whom the elephant appears "will usually find
themselves in a position where the opportunity to reestablish powerful
family and societal ideals will occur." In *Animal-Wise,* Andrews states,
"Zebras teach us individuality within group settings. . . . [and] can show us
ways of working and understanding group dynamics and communications
more clearly. . . . When the zebras appear, examine your relationship to

various groups in your life. Do not confront directly unless there is no other choice. Use your mental agility to work around problems and obstacles, especially if it is in the form of other people and competitors."

On a much broader, collective level, this dream seems to be speaking of one of the most serious problems our world faces, the damage we humans are inflicting upon the environment. As anthropologist Hank Wesselman has pointed out in his book *Medicinemaker,* many scientific studies show that climate changes are warming polar regions, melting ice shelves, and causing the oceans to rise. Most scientists agree that this is being caused by increased atmospheric concentrations of carbon dioxide and other heat-trapping gases, the result of our industrialized society. They warn that if serious measures are not taken immediately to reverse this process there will be an ecological catastrophe that will destroy life as we know it. If the east Antarctic ice sheet slips into the southern oceans, a tidal wave of incredible height could sweep every coastline and take out every port in the world.

The people in the above dream seemed to be experiencing such a catastrophe. I received a warning not just for myself, but also for humanity. One part of the dream's scenario seems unlikely, that one would survive the full impact of such a tidal wave. Dreams bring messages about which something can be done. What can we do? Surely the point is that individually and collectively we must do everything reasonably possible to prevent such a disaster.

In 2003, people in my dreams still were not listening:

Someone Wants Me to Warn People of an Impending Disaster

I've gone to a building to get out of stormy weather. I find lots of other people there. Someone questions why I'm there. I say I've just taken refuge from the weather. I receive a phone call from someone I don't know. The person has heard of me and is begging me to warn other people about an impending disaster. I ask what s/he is talking about. The person says it's what was in the newspaper and it will happen in two days. I then remember seeing the article referred to. After getting off the phone, I turn to people near me and try to tell them what was said. No one wants to pay any attention.

But in fact it is urgent that we all pay attention. In 2003, the world had just experienced the widespread effects of the Asian tsunami, caused by an undersea earthquake. Shortly before I had this last-mentioned dream, P.M.H. Atwater, researcher and author who has written extensively on near-death experiences, reincarnation, and related phenomena, wrote in the Charlottesville area monthly newspaper, *Echo,* the following:

> "The island of La Palma in the Canaries north of Africa is separating—three more feet of recent date. An eruption would cause half of the island to fall into the Atlantic Ocean creating a tsunami wave that would devastate the entire eastern seaboard of the United States, not to mention areas in Canada, Europe, and other countries."

Was this the article I was referring to in the dream?

Global warming may ultimately cause this kind of phenomenon. The earth is already showing signs of the ice cap recession, with the breaking off of glaciers. With this and the melting of snow fields worldwide, we will see a rise in sea level that is predicted to flood seaports and coastal areas worldwide in the coming years. This would have the same effect as the potential tsunami Atwater mentioned.

At the time of the dream, the economic and political leadership in the United States had not taken the threat seriously enough to take the necessary steps to avert this catastrophe, or even to plan how to deal with the situation if it should happen. Individual and national greed and desires for short-term benefits and pleasures derived from the damaging environmental practices blind us to the greater long-term suffering.

In 2004, the dangers had not gone away. Two dreams the same night cried out to be noticed. The first dream:

We Join Many Others Watching the Sky Waiting for Someone's Appearance

Apparently something drastic has happened and my family and I are told that we will have to move. The news bearer is apologetic, saying he understands this will be quite a strenuous undertaking for us. I agree that it will be, but I'm resigned to the inevitable. I begin thinking of the need to take only a fraction of our belongings in the move.

Next I'm standing on a hillside looking skyward and see a huge transport plane overhead. I'm concerned by how low it is, as it goes from my right to the left. I can see that the plane lands somewhere below, perhaps beside a highway, not at an airport.

Then, as my family and I drive down from the hill, we see many people standing out on surrounding hillsides looking up expectantly, wondering what is taking place, seemingly waiting for something. We circle around and stop on a level area part way to the valley, then get out and stand watching and waiting, as are the others. I get the feeling that we are waiting for some "authority" to appear below to make pronouncements to the multitudes that are waiting there.

I awakened with a feeling of unease, almost an ominous dread. I managed to go back to sleep, then five hours later I awoke from this next dream:

I Become Fearful After Overhearing the Men's Conversation

My husband and I have gone into a hotel in an unidentified place to await the arrival of a group of people. At first I'm thinking this group is part of my family, but when they arrive it's obvious they are unknowns. A woman and at least two men walk into our room. The woman sits on my bed, then gets right up and hastily walks back out. The men follow her and we follow them. As we come up to them I overhear conversation between the men and I catch the word "infinity." I become concerned. . . .

I call my husband to me and tell him I'm worried and ask if he heard what the men were talking about. Did he hear the word "infinity"? Yes, he heard and he immediately says it's their word for the end of the world. This is exactly what has worried me. I take it to mean that they belong to a group that is involved in secret affairs, perhaps something we have read about. I'm alarmed and don't want to have anything to do with them. After I hear my husband's response, I leave and return to our room. . . .

The first dream of this night recounted a displacement of people similar to what happened during Hurricane Katrina, even to evacuation by means of large planes. Was this dream a warning of something that could happen in the future? The dream occurred nineteen months before Katrina.

The second dream did not spell out a particular catastrophic event. However, it did point to a deep unconscious fear, one that was growing in my consciousness, of a possible end result of a crisis we are facing. I noted in my journal that the dream had the flavor of espionage and the *DaVinci Code*. When I studied my dream journals, I recalled that these two dreams came during a period when I was experiencing some stressful health issues, but nothing as drastic as the scenarios of these dreams. The dreams might be simply exaggerating my anxiety feelings or expressing my feelings of lack of control in my personal life. Maybe I was also alarmed about our collective crisis.

Six weeks later I had this dream:

We're Trying to Make a Journey Even Though
Things May Become Impossible

Other people and I have been preparing to travel somewhere, evidently on foot. We are told that

At some point I'm out in the town (I don't recall the reason why). As I head back to our home, I see many people beginning to leave. Everyone is walking, carrying what little he or she can manage. Apparently we are not able to use our vehicles. I begin to try to figure out what I—we—need to take with us. Owen and I confer with each other and agree there will likely be times when we will get very cold, so we must take warm clothes. I think of many other items it would be helpful to have with us—additional clothing, bedding, and medicines. (I don't think of food.) However, I tell myself I can't take everything because it would be cumbersome to manage so much; we'll have to walk endlessly and will get exhausted even carrying very little. I then decide I can take just what will fit on my walker. I don't know how we'll get along for very long. To be realistic, we won't.

At some point, after I realize the boy has actually let loose the toxin, I try to point out to others the areas we must avoid as we make our way out of the town. Something about the situation has the feel of a game of hide and seek with the boy. However, the details of this have faded in recall.

The parts that echo some of the earlier scenarios are the need to evacuate our homes and town, worrying about what to take with us, leaving on foot, and the hopelessness of the situation.

I depicted the serious environmental problems in the earlier dreams as being the consequences of damage inflicted by thoughtless, uncaring, and greedy humans. This last dream stated the danger was set in motion by a teenage boy. My take on this is the teenager is a symbol for corporate executives who are behaving like immature teenagers who act without considering the serious consequences of their actions. These executives are thinking only of the profits they can make, it doesn't matter that their actions will lead to catastrophic destruction of the earth's environment. This current dream states the teenager has already set in motion the catastrophe—let loose a toxin—and "is very gleeful and delighted" and the situation has "the feel of a game of hide and seek with the boy." One additional thought: The fact that we are unable to use our vehicles may suggest the country's oil/gas resources have given out, therefore there is no gas available to fuel the vehicles.

I believe, as does dream analyst Jeremy Taylor, all dreams come to help us in some way. He states that no dream—not even the most terrifying ones—ever comes to say, "you have these problems, but you can't do anything about them!" This means that the dreammaker—the divine within us—believes that if we take seriously this all-important problem, there are things we can do to prevent a catastrophe. We must work together to eliminate toxic substances from all areas of our environment and to find new sustainable and environmentally sound resources, while maintaining the ecological balance of nature, even if it means sacrificing personal and corporate gains.

I believe these dreams are saying, "Wake up, everyone, before it's too late!" There's a crisis in the making. Let's work together to save our world.

—14—

MORE ABOUT WATER IN DREAMS

David C. Lohff in *The Dream Dictionary* points out, "Water is central to the human story. Whether it is the deep, fresh lake, the river that brings life, or the ocean that must claim her dead, water is both friend and enemy at once. When dreams contain this powerful image in any of its forms, understanding the role of the water is essential. . . . Water has symbolic, archetypal meaning in that it either provides life or harbors mystery and danger."

Water can symbolize the flow of life energy or one's spiritual conditions (represented by a river), the unconscious (the ocean), and emotions. The forms it takes in our dreams—still or rough, hot or cold, clear or muddy, liquid, frozen, or steam—give us clues as to its meaning. Also, notice whether it is a small man-made lake or a large, natural body of water such as an ocean. The former might represent the personal unconscious, while the latter might be an archetypal symbol for the *collective unconscious* (Carl Jung's term for the basic functional elements of the human psyche common to all cultures).

Think of the many metaphors related to water we use in our everyday speech: "smooth sailing," "shipwrecked individual," "being at sea," "being adrift," "being in hot water," "being up a creek," "going with the flow," "swimming against the current," "the tide has turned," "being on thin ice," and "having broken the ice." When these images appear in our dreams, their metaphorical meanings are likely to be the same as those intended in speech.

Storms

Many dreamworkers agree that an approaching storm in a dream might suggest a building up of tensions and emotions around us or within us. The strength of the storm might indicate the size and force of this inner turmoil—whether we're mildly upset by a disappointment or feeling intense anger over being seriously wronged.

For many years I repeatedly had dreams of approaching storms. Many times the storm passed by or dissipated without causing major damage. This might suggest some situations that appeared to be building up emotionally either did not materialize or were not problematical. Even so, one still wishes to take precautions when warned of an approaching storm. In one dream I was

Escaping an Approaching Storm by Going Down into the Basement

> I am in a house with other people, including my
> husband. . . . I look out a window and see dark clouds
> and a funnel cloud. . . . I call out to everyone to head
> to the basement. . . . I have no memory of anything
> happening while there. We come back up and look to see
> where the storm is. It has passed us by, did not hit us.

The year before, I had a very similar dream of ushering others down into a basement to safety. Since all characters in my dream can represent parts of myself, I was guiding various parts of myself into the unconscious. I need to look for additional clues as to what was going on in my unconscious. In the quoted dream, I didn't recall what happened in the basement. Maybe I blocked the memory, not yet being ready to deal with the problem. In another dream a year earlier I did relate some of what I found in the basement.

Seeking Safety from Storm in a Wet Basement

> . . . As I go down the stairs I feel my feet getting wet,
> but I believe we have no other choice for a protected

place. I go over to a corner or what I think is a corner. The whole basement is dark and we can't see. We just have to feel our way. In a bit I go back up and outside to look at the sky again. It still looks threatening, so I hurry back in and down into the basement. I huddle in a different place that seems like a corner to me. The floor has several inches of water in it. It is a miserable situation, but this is the safest place we can find. Later after the threat has passed and it becomes light, I discover the spot I thought was a corner was more like a place beside a small embankment. There is a stranger—a male—near me as we stand around. I feel the need of consolation and comforting and this person has his arm around me. I lean against him for comfort. . . .

"The basement is dark and we can't see." By definition, we can't see what is in our unconscious. "We just have to feel our way." We have to make use of our feelings. Water is often a symbol for emotions. The floor of this basement was covered with water. I felt miserable and needed comforting. Why I was uncomfortable with emotions and with which emotions in particular? What circumstances led to these emotions? In these dreams I sought safety by going into a basement. This seems to point out the advisability of seeking helpful insights regarding troubling situations by going into one's unconscious. We can do this through the study/exploration of dreams.

Additional questions I can ask myself: What does a small embankment mean to me? Do I have any memory or association that tells of its significance? Maybe it was saying that at least twice I have backed myself into a corner and in one I found a stranger. Who was this stranger? The man was a part of me, my *animus*. He was there to help me and comfort me. Have I been afraid to acknowledge and accept masculine attributes within myself, parts that I need to become a whole person?

Even if the storm passes by, we can benefit and learn something by taking precautions. By paying attention to and taking appropriate action following warning dreams one can possibly forestall, circumvent, or clear up an as yet unrecognized problem. In waking life, storms can clear the air.

Huge Waves

The symbolism of waves is similar to that of storms. The size and type of wave can suggest the strength of the incoming emotions. They might be gentle waves, signifying an emotion is just coming into consciousness. However, a huge wave might suggest the threat of being overcome by an intense emotion—perhaps anger, fear, or despair.

Over a period of fifteen years a recurring theme for me dealt with rough waters, usually waves in an ocean. In an early dream in 1992,

There's a Huge Wave Coming Towards My Boat

. . . In the distance there is a huge swell in the water. Someone in another boat is saying he doesn't want to be where that huge wave will break. It is to my right and getting larger. The dream shifts before anything happens.

I might have been sensing the potential for an emotional upheaval. The fact that the dream shifted before the wave broke might suggest I did not fully recognize or acknowledge the problem or it had not yet fully materialized. The dream pointed out that part of me, the person in the other boat, didn't want to experience the problem.

The next year I dreamed that my son and I were at the seashore when

Water Knocks Russ Over at the Seashore

. . . It is peaceful and beautiful. . . . As I am walking back along the shoreline, everyone in the vicinity yells. They see a huge wave or wall of water headed towards land. They are calling Russ' (our son's) name. I turn and look and see him wash up. He looks up and flops. Next I see he is on his feet and he is embracing a girl.

The initial peacefulness of the scene suggested that life had been going smoothly when an unexpected problem involving our son erupted. We unconscious material in the same way tidal waves do. They may also indicate being overwhelmed by circumstances in waking life. In one of my earliest recorded dreams, from twenty years ago,

I Seek Sanctuary from Flood Waters of a Storm

I am climbing into my room or space somehow to
find sanctuary "out of the storm." I believe there are
floodwaters all around. People may be wondering where
I am, but I think they know I am here. I may leave my
room at least once, but I return again the same way.

I dreamed this early one morning after being awake for several hours during the night, during what had been a very emotional time. Several months before this I had a dream in which my psyche seemed to want to avoid being overcome by emotions. Here is that dream:

Deciding Against a Lot in a Flood Plain

I'm in a strange place for the purpose of finding a good
piece of land on which to build a home. We like the idea
of building in this area near someone we already know.
We go "down the road" or out away from this person's
house looking. The property is beautiful. In many ways
we like it. But then we realize it is in a valley and that in
a certain situation the place would become flooded. We
decide this is not the right place to build.

In subsequent years there were other dreams with a similar theme. In 1998,

I Don't Want to Build a House Surrounded by Water on Three Sides

I am aware of a house (or some other type of building)
located at the edge of water. In fact, it is surrounded by
water on three sides. I feel this is a precarious position

because there may be an embankment at the back with an ocean beyond. I envision waves of water crossing over the edge of the embankment in storms. I decide I would not want to build a home in such a location.

In 1999,

I Wonder If the Building Can Withstand the Force of the Water

I am standing in front of a very large window being shown the view by an unidentified man. In one way the view is magnificent. It is of an ocean. At the same time it is overpowering because the water comes right to the window at eye level. It is then deflected to the left side. I wonder how the building stands up against the force of the water. I assume the building was built with steel beams. Someone asks me if I would like to live in the room or apartment where we are. I reply that the view is magnificent, but I would be very uneasy, wondering if the building would withstand the force of the water as it rolls in.

Then in a dream almost ten years after the first one in this series, I'm still conscious of the potential to experience overwhelming emotions:

I Wonder What We'll Do If Our House Gets Flooded

Owen and I are looking around in what is to be our new home (not the actual one in waking life). I'm not sure in recall whether we have already moved in or not. I become aware that the area is prone to flooding in such a way that one section of our house could possibly be flooded. I voice my concern asking, "What will we do when the floods come?" I can envision water becoming several feet deep in one end of the house. Owen replies, "We'll just have to deal with that if it comes."

This kind of dream often shows us our fears of not making the grade, not being prepared, being incapable of handling some circumstances, or not measuring up to other people's expectations. At the beginning of the dream I felt confident about my progress in the class. I knew enough to be helping another student, but when confronted with a test I was confused and unprepared. I wonder what was happening in my life at the time of the dream for which I felt unprepared. What was I confused about? Was I being expected to do something I did not feel capable of doing? It appeared I was willing to try to do whatever, but I felt overwhelmed by it.

Eight and a half years later I had a similar dream in which I, along with other students, was being given instructions about taking a test. I thought the test paper's size was not adequate.

I'm Upset Because I Failed to Take the Test

> . . . Others are beginning to work on the test and I'm
> still fiddling around. . . . I still haven't even looked at
> the questions. I fear I'll not even get well under way
> and the time will be up. I wake up feeling very uneasy,
> worried about not succeeding at the test. I go back to
> sleep and dream I'm telling my family about my failure
> to take the test. I'm very upset. I fear I'll fail the course
> and will not be able to get my degree. I worry that
> this will keep me from being able to do whatever I'm
> supposed to do. . . .

Undoubtedly many things happened in the intervening years, so perhaps circumstances were different the second time around. But I still had anxieties about what I was doing. In both dreams I worried about time running out. Perhaps I had become aware of my advancing age and I was worried about not having much time left to accomplish whatever I feel I am supposed to do. However, this type of dream can come to anyone at any stage of life. Children can have great anxieties over tests at school.

I evidently felt unprepared for some undertaking facing me. But in a subsequent dream *I'm Told I've Completed the Class Successfully*. The earlier stressful dreams of tests on one level indicated a lack of confidence about some aspect of my life. This last dream was a compensatory dream, reassuring me that I was successfully completing preparatory tasks and I could stop worrying.

Sports

Sports can include activities participated in for recreation, for exercise, and as competitions, undertaken alone, with a partner, or on a team. Almost everyone enjoys these activities as participants and/or spectators, and concepts related to sports and games are part of our psyches. We use sports-related phrases in our everyday speech, such as saying things are "on the ball" or are "right on target." We may "reel someone in" to our way of thinking. We "wrestle with" or "bat around" ideas. We have made a "touchdown" when we have succeeded in some way.

Our dreams may use many of the same figures of speech metaphorically. Ask yourself what you associate with the image or metaphor in the dream. Your own associations are the most important clues to the dream's message. But if you can't think of anything, you can look up the symbol in one of the good dream dictionaries. For instance, regarding *games,* Tanner says, "*Games* can represent the 'game of life' people play with one another and whether or not they play according to the rules. Games have to do with learning the rules, talents, skills, aims, goals, competition, showmanship, practice, training, accuracy, winning or losing, and how we play the game. This includes harmony and cooperation or the lack of it, teamwork, fairness, and good sportsmanship."

I have never been an athletic woman, yet at age 65 I had the following dream:

I Agree to Play Tennis Even Though I'm Not Really a Player

An unidentified man asks me to play tennis. I declare I'm not really a tennis player, but I'm willing to bat the ball around on the tennis court with him for a while, if he understands I'm not really a player. I go to get my racket.

In the context of this dream I might consider a tennis ball to represent an idea. Thus I could be agreeing to hit—toss—ideas back and forth from my court to a man's court. The man might be someone I interacted with in waking life and whose opinions I valued. He might also represent masculine aspects of myself that can help me consider and evaluate ideas.

In another dream

I Have Doubts Whether I Should Have Volunteered to Play Ball

> I have recently moved to a new place. I learn that the people there (perhaps those in a supervisory capacity) would like for all women to participate on a softball team for the area. It is not obligatory, but it is very much desired. I decide I will join the team and am greeted with great enthusiasm. As I'm getting ready to participate, I wonder if I really should be doing this. I know I'm not skilled in the game. I suspect they'll see this as soon as I attempt to play. I'm not even sure I'll be able to hit the ball. I'm signing up to play to let them know I'm willing to do what I can to help out. But I'll probably need to drop out after one time at bat. Would it have been better not to volunteer to begin with?

In the dream I believed I had an altruistic motive for agreeing to join the team, to be a "team player." However, I wonder whether I had other unconscious motives. I can ask myself several questions: First, what in my waking life might be of a similar nature? What are my motives for fulfilling other people's expectations? Am I fearful of being considered deficient in some respect? Am I seeking approval and disregarding my own realistic limitations and needs?

My husband reported the following dream:

Exuberant Joy of Running

> For many years I have had occasional dreams in which I
> am running, not fearfully or away from some danger, and

not in any sort of competition, but by myself and typically in a natural, outdoor setting. The setting is not always well defined, but always is pleasant, and often seems to be a sort of rolling countryside, maybe along a trail of some kind. I am running in a cross-country manner, though without any specific destination. I am typically running relatively fast, not sprinting, but faster than jogging. I am running with ease, long strides, no shortness of breath, a feeling of having ample energy and being able to keep running a long way, a great sense of freedom, as though I could fly. Typically in these dreams I feel happy, even exuberant. I feel happy on waking up, sometimes with the thought that I should do some running again, as years ago I did.

When asked about his additional thoughts and feelings about this dream, Owen said the dream reminded of how he felt in his early childhood, times when he would dress each morning eagerly anticipating running outside to play in his yard and the surrounding natural setting. He was full of exuberance and the joy of living. Something changed when he became seriously ill in the first grade and he has seemed to be seeking to regain this joy ever since. If this were my dream, I would feel that my dreammaker was trying to tell me that the zest for life is still a part of me, awaiting release from within, if I will do whatever I can to make this possible. Possibly, the act of running or other forms of exercise might be a part of this renewal, as well as good for my health.

Our dreams can contain many additional sport symbols, including references to basketball, golfing, fishing, bicycling, skating, etc. When they appear, ask yourself what are the chief characteristics of the game or activity. Then see how these might refer to something in your life. For instance, when you are bicycling, you must keep your balance and move under your own power. In the dream, were you having trouble doing this? If so, what was out of balance in your waking life?

Holiday Experiences

In the past, holidays were considered to be happy times for everyone. Time to share warm fellowship and delicious meals with family and friends. Time

there is something we can do to improve our situation. It is up to us to figure out how we can best do this.

Puns and Metaphors

Occasionally our dreammakers like to use puns—either verbal puns (homophones) or pictorial/visual puns.

Verbal puns using *homophones* are words that are spelled differently but sound the same, such as plane/plain, dear/deer, and dye/die. If you dream something about a plane, it might be suggesting that you are feeling rather plain. (Or it might not.) If you see a deer (a hoofed animal with antlers) in your dream, you might be thinking of someone who is dear (of value) to you.

Pictorial or visual puns use visual images to communicate a metaphor. If you have a dream in which you see a horseman riding on the roofs of buildings, it might suggest that you are "riding your high horse." A dream of a person doing something in a tent might suggest that the dreamer is "intent" on doing something.

Some years ago I had the following dream:

On Thin Ice

I'm on a pond that is frozen over. Lots of people are there. Some are emergency workers. I don't remember exactly what is going on. What I do remember is that as I am walking off the ice I poke the ice with a thin stick or rod that easily produces a small hole, letting water come through. As I do this I call out a warning to the people around: "You're on thin ice. You should hurry off the ice. It's dangerous."

The meaning of this seems fairly obvious. We all know the expression "you're on thin ice." I was being asked to consider what about my life might be dangerous in some way. It didn't necessarily imply it was a physical danger. The "danger" might be mental, spiritual, or physical, or all of these.

Pictorial puns might not always be humorous or pleasant. Back in 1997 I had a dream that horrified me. This is the dream:

There's a Kitten in a Stew

> . . . I am visited by family, which in the dream includes small children. I have prepared a "stew" for a meal, but probably have not expected this company. I am alarmed to see the children, especially a little girl, for I know she would be alarmed to see what is in the stew. I hastily go to the kitchen and pull something out of the stew. What I pull out is a kitten's head, with skin dangling. The body part has already "cooked down" into the stew.

What a gruesome image, especially for a cat lover, as I am! Animals—beloved pets in particular—can sometimes be symbols for oneself. I have often dreamed of kittens as symbols for myself. In this dream the kitten was in a stew. Here is a visual representation to communicate a metaphor. Remember, too, that all images in a dream represent parts of oneself. I was the cook who put the kitten in the stew, I was the kitten in the stew, and I was the child whom I wanted to protect from the sight of what was in the stew by taking the kitten out of the stew. Since I was the one who created the stew, I can also get myself out of it. The dream was offering me the opportunity to figure out what had upset me and to work with my deeper Self to get myself out of the "stew."

In the following dream the reference to food seems to be just part of a pun.

I'm Taking a Group Their Just Desserts

> I'm with others (I forget where). I'm helping provide refreshments. I take platters of desserts—cookies, pastries, etc.—to the group gathered in the adjoining room. In recall, I think to myself that I'm taking them "just desserts." They are getting their "just desserts."

In order to understand this dream I can try to figure out what waking life circumstances this might be referring to. Was there a situation that upset me and possibly might have caused me to feel this way about a particular group? What might I be able to do to improve the situation and my feelings about it?

George R. Slater in *Bringing Dreams to Life* states, "The meaning of a dream may . . . be conveyed by a pun or an absurdity. In my experience, these are not very frequent and when they do occur we are more likely to stumble upon them accidentally or have them pointed out by another person than to decode them ourselves. It does help to let your imagination go free in stating any sayings or near-word likenesses that connect with the dream."

If you can't figure out the meaning of your dream, it might be very helpful to read it out loud several times, listening carefully to every word and group of words. Think of a second or third meaning of notable images in the dream. Or ask yourself what other way you might say the same thing, such as "What is a horse on a roof?" It's a high horse. These humorous images can lead us to possible meanings. Dreams often emphasize by exaggeration. So even gruesome images are pointing out important messages from our inner selves. Listen! Pay attention. Then follow up with some "action"—physical, mental, or symbolic—that will help you in your journey towards wholeness.

Pre-Election Dreams

How did a dream of mine recorded in November 2002 have anything to do with the Election of 2004? Back then, I had no idea that it did. Some understanding of the dream's significance came 21 months later after having another dream that I decided must be connected. Here's the first dream:

I Visit a Mysterious Place Along with Other People

I'm visiting some "establishment"—looking around the large building housing the "place." There's a large room that seems to have various spaces used for different purposes. One side is fitted out with rows of seats like church pews. A small area opening onto this seems to be used differently—I see couches and tables. Beyond this is a doorway leading into an area evidently not open to the public.

I'm there with unidentified people. We begin to sense that the place is used for some secret purpose. We are not allowed to explore beyond this "open" area. I say I think even this area with rows of seats, which we are led to assume is a church, has another purpose. I don't know what. There are "officials" standing to the side overseeing the visit and keeping us from exploring beyond this area. If anyone should try to explore farther, we all would be asked to leave.

When we do leave the building, we're surprised to discover that the road into the place has been destroyed—we assume to keep others out. We have to figure a way to get out by finding a path our vehicle can travel. As we get to the edge of the property, we find a vehicle about to enter. I feel we need to warn them about what they may find.

Dreams are messages from our inner selves, drawing background material from our lives and our personal and the collective unconscious. Dreams always have multiple meanings and layers of significance. They can deal with our physical health, emotional and psychological status, spiritual life, and relationships with other people. They may also be bringing into consciousness a collective issue or circumstance.

At the time of this dream there was nothing going on in my personal life to which this dream seemed to refer. But considering a "building" to be a symbol for one's self, perhaps this dream was pointing out that there was a part of me not open to the public, a part that I keep private. This certainly is true, I already was aware of this. But dreams come to bring new understandings, not to point out what you already know. I put the dream aside and hoped further illumination would come later. It came with this next dream in early September 2004:

While Helping Prepare the "Dance" Floor, I Worry about the Proposed "Game of War"

> I'm with an unidentified person in a public gathering
> place. We're helping clean/prepare some type of dance/
> recreation space. We are required to do this. I'm
> complaining to my companion about the situation.
> Evidently the men in charge are proposing some type of
> "game" in which others will be required to participate.
> It is a "game of war." I say I don't understand how they
> can want to do this. It will involve serious consequences
> for so many people. My companion agrees with me.

My immediate association to "the men in charge" requiring others to participate in a "game of war" that will "involve serious consequences for so many people" was our government and our involvement in Iraq. Now there's the connection to the 2004 Election.

I decided to look back through my dream journals for other dreams of authority figures, dreams that might be connected to this dream. That's when I saw anew the November 2002 dream recounted above. In it I visited "some establishment" which we sensed "is used for some secret purpose" where "we are not allowed to explore beyond this 'open' area" and "officials" were "overseeing the visit and keeping us from exploring beyond this (open) area." I now consider this a reference to the then current administration's policies of secrecy and deception in place in 2002. Examples materialized as it became evident that the real reason for waging war in Iraq was hidden and denied. Decisions and deals with war profiteers were shrouded with secrecy behind closed doors, and the photographs of consequences of the war (dead soldiers, body bags, and coffins) were banned from public view.

In the dream I said I thought the area with seats like church pews had another purpose. In waking life I believe the faith-based advocacy of the administration at that time was being used to push a right-wing moral agenda and perhaps to support the ideological agenda of the groups to whom support was given. Unfortunately, I think the right-wing ideologues are still pushing their agenda.

Next we "discover that the road into the place has been destroyed—we assume to keep others out." Access to/communication with the government had been destroyed. "We have to figure a way to get out by finding a path our vehicle can travel." We, the people, needed to find a way out of this situation. The second half of the more recent dream suggested a way. It stated:

> Sometime later, after completing our chore, we watch as
> a couple dances around the outside of the special floor
> area where we are standing. I comment on how well
> they are dancing. Then I notice that the woman is much
> older than the man, who appears to be a teenager. She
> is "leading." I comment that she is showing him how to
> dance.

The space we prepared for the game of war had become a dance floor where a couple was engaged in a graceful dance, the dance of life. This is very different from a game of war.

I believe the young male represented our historically young patriarchally dominated nation, one involved in repeated aggressive games of war. I was encouraged to see he was being instructed by the older woman who might represent wise, mature feminine attributes, perhaps even the divine feminine. I hope she was "leading" him back to ways of pre-patriarchal cultures in which people lived without the need of fortifications and weapons, sharing with and caring for all beings.

Dreams come in the service of health and wholeness. In this case not just for an individual but the collective—the whole world. May we as a nation learn the ways of peace.

—16—

ANIMALS IN DREAMS

Animals are common images in our dreams. They may symbolize our basic animal drives, survival instincts, wild hopes and desires. They can also represent our natural urges, intuitions, and playful feelings. In many cases they are unexpressed energies. It is helpful to take note of the particular characteristics of the animal pictured in our dream. Is it a domesticated pet or a wild animal? What are our own ideas about and reactions to the animal in real life as well as in the dream?

Horses

Horses in our dreams may be domesticated—almost pets that we ride and enjoy for pleasure or work animals that help plow fields or pull wagons or coaches providing transportation. Other horses may be wild, untamed creatures. We can ask ourselves what the animal's color is, what it is doing in the dream, and whether we have control over it or it is running wild and perhaps attacking us.

Ted Andrews suggests in his book *Animal-Speak*, "If a horse has shown up in your life, it may be time to examine aspects of travel and freedom within your life. Are you feeling constricted? . . . Is it time to assert your freedom and your power in new areas? . . . Horse brings with it new journeys. It will teach you how to ride into new directions to awaken and discover your own freedom and power."

I had a series of dreams about horses. In three of them I was alarmed by a horse coming towards me. What was I afraid of and did I need to be afraid? Let's see what the horse might have been coming to show me.

In the first dream, which occurred just a few months after my cancer experience,

I Seek Safety When a Wild, Black Stallion Rushes Towards Me

> While at a ranch, out away from the house I see a black
> stallion off in the distance.
>
> I'm told it is a wild one and I should get to the safety
> of the house if it comes close. Some time later I'm
> out by myself and I see the stallion coming my way.
> I go towards the house. The stallion gets closer and is
> rushing, galloping towards me. I run to get up on the
> porch of the house and thus to safety. I seem to just
> make it.

The horse in this dream was black, which suggests unknown or mysterious forces. In waking life, I was recovering from breast cancer and was reassessing my life and pondering new directions I would like to take. The black horse might symbolize my survival instincts, basic animal drives, sub-conscious and untamed desires, possibly my hopes for the future. A part of me was afraid of this wild creature and its energies. But my survival might depend upon my allowing these new creative energies to come into my life and flourish.

Almost five years later, I dreamed

I Fear the Horse Might Run Us Down; My Friend Doesn't

> I am outside with my dearest, lifelong friend. We are
> dancing around joyfully, perhaps as small children
> would do; but we are not children, we're adults. We're
> having a marvelous time. We look across the field and
> see a horse beyond the fence. It is moving towards the
> fence, about to jump it. I'm concerned that we should
> move out of the way—fearful it might run us down. My
> friend is not worried. She stays where she is.

I was having a wonderful time with my lifelong friend. As a dream symbol, this friend represented a part of me that has been with me since childhood, a feminine part of me that has retained the spontaneous joy of a child and whose presence encourages me to exhibit this joy. By staying where she was upon seeing the approaching horse, she showed me I need not fear the creative energies that were rushing towards consciousness.

Two years later, this dream:

We Become Alarmed by the Wild Horse

I'm outside by a field that has a deep ravine in the middle. A woman is out in the middle of this ravine. I see a wild horse charging towards her. This alarms me and others—maybe including my husband—who are out there with me. We hurry to close the gate at the end of a corral to control the horse.

A ravine is a low place. In this dream it was in the middle of a field— perhaps "a field of endeavor." In this dream, I was both the woman in the ravine in the middle of the field and the dreamer. Perhaps I was feeling low (I was in the ravine) about some aspect of my life, some undertaking (field of endeavor). My husband represented my masculine energies that could help me. Together we took action to control the horse, to contain it in the field. Thus I was calling upon both my feminine and masculine attributes. Rather than driving away the horse, we corralled it to keep it contained and possibly make use of its power and basic animal drives.

In looking back at this dream, I speculate that I had kept these basic animal instincts and drives, untamed desires, wild hopes and tendencies, and creative energies repressed in my body for many years. Various life circumstances might have made me think I would be safer not to acknowledge these energies that are within me. The dreams, which originate from the wise, inner depths of my unconscious, came to bring the matter into my consciousness to show me I need not fear these energies. Through mindful awareness they can be contained and channeled into beneficial ways.

These psychic energies that once may have felt threatening can, through the means of dream exploration, be transformed into healing energies on physical, mental, and spiritual levels.

These three dreams show a very positive transition in my psyche. I have allowed new energies into my consciousness—"horsepower" that can help me discover my own freedom and power during my journey towards wholeness.

An Animal as a Symbol for Oneself

Objects, people, and animals are symbols when they show up in your dreams. They may mean different things to different people, depending upon your associations with them. If the person has had a bad experience with a dog or a cat, he or she might feel very negative about such a symbol in a dream. But if the person has had happy experiences with a particular animal, the associations probably will be positive. You might even find such an animal appearing frequently in dreams as a symbol for yourself. This has been true for me. After having many dreams of small kittens and cats over the years, I came to realize that they might be a symbol for myself.

Many years ago I had the following dream:

The Kitten Is in Need of Nourishment and Loving Care

I discover a very tiny kitten covered over by papers or other clutter on a table. I realize that this kitten has been there for a long time and has not received any nourishment for days. I marvel at its ability to still be alive and I carefully pick it up and am going to immediately give it food and loving.

I found this dream to be significant. The dream occurred the night after I attended an art therapy workshop in which I was told that certain tests showed that there was a part of me that needed nurturing and care and that I needed to see to my own needs.

About a year later I had this dream:

The Teacher Is Paying Attention to the Needs of My Kitten

I am going to school and it is an all-day session for
several days in a row. I don't remember whether I stayed
overnight. But I have taken a kitten with me to care for.
I evidently am involved in my schoolwork and am not
paying attention to the kitten. I notice that the teacher
has gotten the kitten and is putting it into a large
covered-over pen made of cardboard. Also she is putting
a litter pan in it for the kitten. I had forgotten to provide
one. I am very pleased the teacher has thought of this
and is concerned for the kitten.

Still another year later I had this dream:

I Need to Care for a Small Kitten As If It Were a Special Child

I pick up a small kitten to care for it as if it were a
special child. I may take it to show an older woman,
maybe my mother.

Four months later:

I Need to Take Care of Tiny Kitten Whose Mother Is Not Around

I'm trying to lead my pets home. One cat is entangled
in a bush. Later I find strange cats in my yard. I bring
one into the house to show someone else. It is just a tiny
kitten. I comment that it is too young to be leaving its
mother. I wonder how I can take care of it. I think I
need to because I don't see its mother around anywhere.

I realized that the first dream in this series pointed out the need to nurture
myself. I saw that the second dream showed me that a year later I was still
not paying enough attention to my own needs. But the following year I

have finally realized the need to take care of myself as "a special child," as, indeed, each one of us is.

There was a reference in both the third and fourth dream to a mother. In the third dream I wanted to show my mother the kitten. In the fourth, the kitten was without its mother and needed to be cared for. Dreams always have more than one level of meaning. If my mother were alive, I might, on one level, simply want to show the kitten to her. On another level, if my mother is deceased, or even if she isn't, the reference could be to the "mothering" part of myself. In actuality, my mother died when I was only 32 years old, many years before I had these four dreams; so in essence, I felt like a motherless kitten. The kitten part of myself, no matter how old I am, needs mothering, nurturing by the maternal part.

Many men are especially fond of dogs. They might then have dreams of puppies and dogs that act as symbols for themselves. Some young teenage females are especially fond of horses, so horses might readily appear in their dreams. But no matter your age or sex, you might dream about many different animals, even ones you know nothing about. If this happens, try to discover the characteristics of the particular animal and observe what it is doing in the dream. This will help you understand what the message of the dream might be.

Next time an animal appears in one of your dreams, the dream might be telling you something on both the literal level and a personal and/or collective metaphorical one. Is the animal acting lively and having a good time or is it cowering before a wild animal or fierce taskmaster? Does it look undernourished or well fed? If there appears to be some area of its life that needs to be changed, consider what can be done for the animal. If you—the dreamer—in the dream are afraid of the animal, perhaps the dream is suggesting you are afraid of the energies within you that the animal represents. Reflect on how these energies might be beneficial and figure out how you can befriend them and incorporate them into your life.

Prehistoric Animals

Several people have suggested that dreams of primitive/prehistoric animals are bringing up issues from very deep within the unconscious. Let's consider a series of dinosaur dreams I had over a period of five and a half years, beginning in July 1994. In the first one I had an

Encounter with the Dinosaur-Like Creature

> I am outside on a big estate with a group of people (women, I think). We are on a path, enjoying the walk and the scenery, which is quite lovely. I don't remember whether I'm with others or am by myself when a huge dinosaur-like creature appears off to one side and is blocking my path. Its head rises up from the dense growth. If I continue on the path it will be able to reach out to where I will pass. Therefore I don't want to continue on that way. I decide I have to find another way.

Because dinosaurs are extinct, they can represent parts of ourselves that are outdated, perhaps something from our past that causes us to be unwilling or unable to adapt to new circumstances. Maybe we need to let go of the past. Perhaps something in it, such as a relationship or a career, is ending and it is now time for us to think more about what is happening in the present. In this dream I feared what would happen if I continued on my current path where the dinosaur could reach me. I didn't want to "continue on that way" and decided to change directions. I needed to decide what about my life, ideas or actions, might obstruct my progress and what changes would be beneficial. Were there emotional or spiritual issues I needed to face and attend to? Since the animal involved was extremely "primitive," it was quite likely that the problem was something buried deep within my unconscious.

Dream analyst Jeremy Taylor points out, "The more menacing or problematic the relationships with animals are in the dream . . . the more likely it is that the dreamer is at odds with his or her instinctive energies, and needs to find a way to channel creative, positive expression of those same instinctive drives into his or her waking life."

A year and a half after the above dream, I had this dream:

I'm Followed by a Strange Animal

> I'm outside. I am being followed by something very
> strange. It almost seems to be a prehistoric animal. At
> first I am fearful, but then it becomes apparent that it
> does not intend harm. In fact it seems to be following
> me in a playful fashion—as would a pet. It is not very
> large—about the size of a three-foot to four-foot high
> boulder.

The fact that the prehistoric animal, which at first seemed to be threatening, had become playful and intended no harm might suggest I had indeed found what Taylor calls "a way to channel creative, positive expression of those same instinctive drives" into my waking life.

Then two and a half years later, I still seemed concerned about these "primitive" instincts. I reported:

I'm Worried About Safety in a Park with a Prehistoric Animal

> I'm outside in a small park when I see a large creature
> the size of an ostrich walking around. It is much heavier
> than an actual ostrich and looks somewhat prehistoric.
> I'm worried about whether it will be hostile and come
> after me. But someone has it under control to prevent it
> from harming me or anyone else around.

My first association to an ostrich is that it is known for burying its head in the sand. This could symbolize someone who deliberately ignores unpleasant events. The animal seemed to me to be some type of prehistoric ostrich, so I think that part of me wanted to avoid paying attention to certain aspects of my life. But "someone (a part of me) had it (the ostrich) under control to prevent it from harming" anyone. So I was becoming aware and taking responsibility for my ostrich-like thoughts, habits, and actions.

Progress in various undertakings is not always continuous. Sometimes we slip backwards. We may see this in our dreams. In the next dream of this series, which came nine months later, I encountered the dinosaur again.

I See a Friend About to Be Eaten by a Dinosaur

> I'm walking outside with a friend. Suddenly a large
> dinosaur appears while I'm walking away from the
> friend. I look back and see the dinosaur has taken my
> friend in its mouth. I see her feet frantically kicking as
> she is being taken up by the huge animal. I hurry over
> to a male friend to tell him what's happening.

My conscious self—the "I"—was frightened by what had happened to my friend (who represented another aspect of myself) when I was not paying attention. I hurried to tell my male friend what happened. In a woman's dreams an unidentified man often represents a hidden inner side of the woman that is assertive, logical, and competitive—her animus. The dream (or my recall of it) ended before any conversation with the friend was revealed. When a situation in a dream is unresolved, the dreamer can ask him/her self what would be the most beneficial ending of the story. In this situation I could enlist the man's aid to rescue my friend. This would suggest I can call upon my animus (its attributes and energies) whenever I feel overpowered by whatever the dinosaur represented.

Not everyone will dream of dinosaurs. We are more likely to encounter present day animals—domestic and wild. We can still use the same process of considering the animals' characteristics, our reactions to the animals, what is going on in our everyday life, and the circumstances within the dream to help decipher the messages the animals bring by their presence. They are coming to us in our dreams to help us learn about ourselves while we're on our life's journey, a journey towards wholeness.

Snakes

Snake dreams can be very difficult dreams to understand, especially if you have little knowledge of the wide variety of cultural traditions regarding snakes.

For people who fear snakes in waking life, a snake dream may seem to be a frightening nightmare. But the snake is not a sign to be feared. In ancient Greek and Roman cultures it was a symbol for healing. Today two intertwined snakes on Hermes' staff, the Caduceus, is the symbol of the medical profession.

We can learn much from someone like Ted Andrews who has in-depth knowledge of historic and mythic lore of various cultures, as well as many years of personal experience and encounters with multiple aspects of nature.

Andrews in his book *Animal-Wise* tells us, "Most traditions around the world. . . taught that the animals we fear are also our potential totem guides. Our fears and doubts take the form of an animal, and until we come to terms with them, we are not whole. . . . Every tradition also taught that if we dream of an animal, it is the same as having actually encountered it while awake. We need to treat the appearance of an animal in our dreams just as significantly. We should study it. The nice thing about dream animals is that by looking at where the dream scenario took place and who else was in it, we can get an idea as to what part of our life this animal applies."

In the Bible, the snake symbolizes temptation and forbidden knowledge. Sigmund Freud considered it a symbol for sexuality. Carl Jung considered it an archetypal representation of the essential energy of life and nature.

Andrews says, "All venomous animals teach us something about the toxicity and poisons in our life. They help point to paths of healing for us. . . . They sometimes appear to awaken our own innate healing energies and abilities."

Soon after I completed radiation therapy for breast cancer in 1994 I dreamed of encountering a copperhead while outside in a wooded area.

Picking Up a Copperhead

I am concerned about there being snakes around.
Possibly I hear, then I see, something that I pick up.
Sure enough, it is a snake. I know it could possibly bite
me while I'm holding it. Even though I try to hold it
so it won't bite me, it does—on my right hand near the

knuckles. This is the hand I'm holding it with. Next I wonder how to get rid of it. If I let go, it'll be loose in the woods and could bite someone else; but I don't think of killing it, just getting it out of my hand so it won't bite me again. So I simply drop the snake and assume it slithers away. I suck my hand, trying to get the venom out and then go hunt for a telephone to call for help. The snake is rather small and not very long, not more than two feet. In thinking about the dream, I hear the word "copperhead" in my mind. I wonder if the name copperhead is significant—"copper head"—since I'm a redhead.

I had been very worried about the advisability of the radiation treatment. Perhaps I feared it was a snake-in-the-grass that might be hurtful. In the dream I didn't want to kill the snake, but I didn't want to be bitten (poisoned) again.

My understanding of dreams was very limited at the time I dreamed this snake dream. When I came back to this dream years later, I was fascinated to learn what Andrews had to say about copperheads.

Andrews explains, "When encountered, many poisonous snakes will alert and warn, and even move out of the way if they feel they will be disturbed. The copperhead rarely moves on. It will stand its ground, expecting the intruders to go around it. If disturbed, it will attack rather than move. The copperhead brings a message of standing one's ground, even if only based upon a 'feeling' . . . . When the copperhead appears, it is usually an indication we need to get more assertive and aggressive in our healing and other activities."

As the messenger, the copperhead was saying I should stand my ground, to stand by my feelings about various healing procedures. This message came after I had already made the necessary decisions regarding my treatments; however, I had intuitively stood by my feelings. Perhaps this dream came to affirm my decisions.

Also, I asked myself, "What needed to be healed?" My first response was the cancer. I then questioned what in my life might have contributed to my illness. What changes might promote healing and prevent further problems? The snake renews itself by shedding its old skin. New growth is possible only after shedding—shedding old beliefs and ways—to embrace a new path in life, possibly one of discovering one's own innate healing energies and abilities.

Eight months later I had a similar dream:

After Swimming Across a River I'm Bitten by a Snake

> To complete my "journey". . . , I plunge into a river and swim to the far bank. As I pull myself up onto the far side I'm bitten on my little finger of my left hand. Again I seek help. . . .

Plunging into a river can be a metaphor for going into the personal unconscious and I was doing this as I continued my "journey," the journey of life. I think the dream showed I had been undertaking the quest suggested by the earlier dream and I was being reminded to keep at it.

Six months later I had this dream:

I Warn We Must Be Careful Where We Step

> I am outside walking with a friend. We see our destination up ahead of us and there is a passageway to our left through which we need to walk. There is a thick covering of leaves on the ground. As I look down I see, partially exposed and partially under the leaves, what looks like a snake with a diamond pattern. I warn the person with me that we must be very careful where we step. But I do not say we must not go on past where I have seen the snake.

In this dream I was aware of the presence of a rattlesnake, but I was not harmed by it. I was intent upon continuing on my path, being aware of the snake with its message, and was beginning to understand my inner visions and dreams and new opportunities for healing which were opening for me. But a little over a month later

I See a Snake Among the Vines

> I look out a window and think I see a small snake
> nestled among the vines. As I watch for a while I
> realize it is a large, long snake. Clydesdale is out there
> somewhere. I'm concerned that he'll tangle with the
> snake.

Clydesdale was one of my pet cats; he could be a symbol for myself. Obviously I was still concerned and on the alert. But the snake could simply be appearing to keep me mindful of all I was learning and needed to do to keep myself healthy and on a healing path.

Just a few weeks ago, 18 years after the first dream of this series and 12 and a half years after the above dream, I was intrigued to have another dream of a snake. What was especially interesting was that the snake was no longer a threat. The snake appeared in the second half of the dream:

We Offer the Pet Snake a Treat

> . . . Then at some point I'm in a room where we discover
> a snake curled up, and perhaps sleeping, on a shelf or
> on the top of a small dresser. We don't want to disturb
> it. Although we are startled when we see it, we know
> it is considered a pet. So much so we decide to give
> it a treat—something to eat—before leaving. I get
> something (don't know what) and hold it near the snake.
> It evidently becomes aware that the food is there and
> it uncurls enough to move its head over to the food.
> It seems to "sniff" it and then turns away. We decide
> it doesn't want what was offered. We now feel we can
> leave. At least we offered the snake something. . . .

All dreams are concerned with our inner transformations. I feel this last dream showed there has indeed been a transformation. The snake was now considered a pet that should be offered a treat. My dreammaker acknowledges the snake is a symbol of healing and it was coming in the service of health and wholeness.

Hearing Animal Voices

Periodically over a span of many years, I had startling dreams in which an animal or insect spoke to me with a human voice. Here is one from 1992:

The Hornet with a Human Face Assures Me It Is Not Dangerous

> I am in a room in the house where a huge insect, a
> gigantic hornet, flies in the door. Considering the hornet
> dangerous, I begin swinging at it with a broom. Then,
> after a bit, the hornet begins to speak to me. I notice
> it has a human-like face. It assures me that it is not
> dangerous. It says it understands how I would think it
> is, but it is not going to hurt me.

Some years later I read several books by animal communicators. They told of amazing "conversations" with animals and insects. I am intrigued by the similarity of some of the reported experiences to the dream above.

J. Allen Boone tells in his groundbreaking book *Kinship With All Life,* written over 50 years ago, of his communication with ants, flies, dogs, and skunks. Through his close association with Strongheart, a German shepherd dog who was a leading Hollywood screen star in the 1920s, Boone learned how to exchange thoughts and feelings with other life forms. He wrote that "various four-legged, six-legged and no-legged fellows shared priceless wisdom with me. They taught me that perfect understanding and perfect co-operation between the human and all other forms of life is unfailing whenever the human really does his required part."

When Boone encountered ants invading his house and icebox, his first impulse was to eradicate them with poison. However, through "intuitive communication" with the ants he set up what he called "a gentleman's agreement" with them and they left his house and never returned.

Communicators explain that the intuitive ways in which humans can both send and receive messages from animals include inner visions, sounds, and feelings.

Although I do not communicate with animals in the way these communicators do, perhaps my dreams are initiating a similar phenomenon. Dreams are an inner knowing, coming to us from our inner Self. Boone referred to this "inner Divinity" as "the Mind of the Universe [that] speaks through a man to his dog and through the dog to the man." This Divinity is within all life and can help establish a mental bridge between life forms. Marta Williams in her book *Learning Their Language* refers to this as "an invisible translator box, metaphorically speaking," that translates intuitive messages into "a form intelligible to the other party." Perhaps my dreammaker, this same inner Divinity, is sending me messages the animals and insects would give me if I were communicating directly.

On another level we can consider all people, animals, and insects in our dreams as symbols representing aspects of ourselves. Thus I needed to figure out what part of myself the hornet represented and what message it was bringing me.

Over the years I have repeatedly dreamed of cats. I understand that these are symbols for myself. In 2001 I had a dream in which I was in a "stranger's" house holding a cat I had recently acquired. I have summarized the dream here:

My Large Cat Speaks

The cat leaps out of my arms and races up the stairs to where some small children have just been put to bed. Since I don't know how the cat acts with children, I'm worried that it might get into their rooms. I call out to warn the adults what has happened. In a minute the man appears with the cat in his arms. He says he was able to catch it easily. He places the cat back in my arms. Later the cat says a word. We are startled. We make additional conversation and *the cat says another single word.*

Later I'm in a public setting, watching as the performers line up for their curtain call. Again, I have the large cat in my arms. After all the bows are over, I'm standing, looking around, perhaps talking with some people, when the cat begins talking—words—full sentences— giving its opinion on something or other.

I next go to another place, perhaps a library, with the cat still in my arms. There are other women seated around the room. They look up as we enter. The cat continues speaking.

Marta Williams says when you hear an animal intuitively, you may get single words or whole phrases. But it's so surprising to hear this you may assume you are making things up. How similar this is to what happened in my dream!

The message I take from this dream is this: Being in a stranger's home signified I was unacquainted with some parts of myself, including children—new, undeveloped talents. I was worried about what I (the cat part of me) might do with these new talents. The man, my masculine attributes from my unconscious, retrieved the cat (the more adventurous and outgoing part of myself) and placed it back in my arms—back under the control of my ego-consciousness. Perhaps the ego wanted to keep too much control. Maybe "the cat" should have been allowed its freedom to go where it wanted, to be with the new talents. The next parts of the dream had the cat beginning to speak in public places, probably surprising those who heard. The cat represented the deep, intuitive part of me that was beginning to find its voice.

Nine years earlier I had a similar dream in which a cat spoke. At the time I found it hard to believe it could speak and I did not encourage it to express itself. I was not ready to recognize this intuitive part of myself or to let it be heard. But many dreams and waking-life events, which have occurred during the intervening years, have awakened me to new ideas and new possibilities. I believe it is time to allow my inner voice to express itself.

The ability to understand dream messages and communications with animals and other life forms is possible for all humans. It does take effort on our part to learn how. Why should we try? Penelope Smith, author of *Animals: Our Return to Wholeness,* suggests that the results of such communication "will change the evolution of the planet. It will change our destroying of the ecosystem into our loving the whole system, loving ourselves as part of the web of life instead of seeing ourselves as separate from nature. As we regain the ability to communicate with all life, we also begin to tap into the great wealth of knowledge that is in all beings."

—17—

BABIES & CHILDREN IN DREAMS

Babies are frequent images in our dreams. In families with a newborn child or where a birth is expected, a dream baby may represent an actual baby. However, the baby also has multiple meanings. It might represent a newly-emerged personality or trait just beginning to become visible, or the product of some creative endeavor —a painting, book, musical creation, or a new project of any kind. Pregnancy can symbolize the incubation period of an idea that is developing in the unconscious. A birth symbolizes a new beginning, a bringing forth of expressions from within.

It is easy to understand how a woman who is pregnant might dream of being pregnant. Such dreams might reveal her happy anticipation of the event, rehearse the actual process—whether natural or caesarean—or reveal her unconscious anxieties about being a competent mother or fears of something going wrong.

During her pregnancy our daughter Marcia shared a special dream with us. In it she dreamed of having a visit from her long-deceased grandmother for whom she was named. She recounted the dream visit as follows:

A Gift of Shoes

Grandmother Marcia has been here, and is now about to leave to go back to wherever she "resides" now. I.e., since she died decades ago, she has come for a special visit from "beyond." Before she leaves she is about to give me a gift. When I see what it is, I think about trying to stop her. She is going to give me a pair of shoes. In my

dream, I am thinking, now that's not going to work.
I don't fit into most of my mother's shoes, since I am
bigger than she is, and my grandmother was much
smaller even than my mother. I remember hearing
that she weighed 98 lbs. when she got married, and I
normally weigh about 60-65 lbs. more than that! So,
I certainly won't fit into any of her shoes. But then I
think, no harm in letting her give them to me. The
shoes are a wonderfully beautiful old-style pump—
pointed toes and fabric covered with raised dots on
them. Something you might see in a fashion museum.
They may be green. I try them on, and amazingly, they
fit me perfectly—so apparently some special quality
makes them work for me.

When asked to elaborate further on the shoes in the dream Marcia said, "They were definitely pointed and covered in fabric. Very tasteful. Not ordinary—definitely extraordinary. Dressy, but not flashy and not just something for evening clothes. If you wore them with daytime clothes, they would make the outfit."

Shoes literally connect us to the ground. Thus, metaphorically they might relate to how we are grounded, our beliefs and how well we can act upon them. "Pumps" (a type of high heel shoes for women) might represent feminine attitudes or a woman's understanding of a female's role in life. In this dream, Marcia was wondering whether she could fit into her grandmother's shoes; she was expressing anxiety about trying to "fill someone else's shoes."

Although Marcia was not sure the shoes were green, they reminded her of my discarded green satin pumps that she had for playing dress up in when she was a child. Green is the color of the heart chakra. *Chakras* refer to "spinning vortices of energy created within us by the interpenetration of consciousness and the physical body," according to Anodea Judith and Selena Vega in *The Sevenfold Journey*. They tell us "the heart chakra is the center of love, compassion, balance, and peace. . . . Love in the fourth chakra is felt as a state of being, emanating from the center and radiating out to all that it encounters. . . . [T]he principle of equilibrium governs the heart chakra. . . . When we enter into balance with ourselves, our relationships, and our environment, we enter a deep sense of serenity and peace."

Since her grandmother died when she was only five years old, Marcia wishes she had more memories of her. She stated, "I guess some qualities I associate with her are gentleness and kindness." She remembers some small ceramic animals she played with when visiting her grandparents not long before her grandmother died.

I recall Mother was especially good with children. She kept little ceramic figurines (the ones Marcia remembers) and perhaps other toys inside a small hexagonal lamp table within the children's reach in their living room. She tried to think of ways to make the children feel accepted and at ease and have fun in their grandparents' home. Recollections of my own childhood: Mother guided my older brother and me with much patience and love through all the joys and tears of growing up—doctoring our skinned knees, sore throats, and childhood diseases; instructing us in social graces and codes of conduct; comforting us when we felt lonely and discouraged; and praising our successes—academic, musical, artistic, and social.

Marcia's dream came when she was five months pregnant, eagerly looking forward to this her first (and only) child. She had been working successfully in the business world for two decades. In contrast, her grandmother's life had centered almost entirely around her family and her husband's job. In the dream Marcia wondered how she could possibly fit into her grandmother's shoes, which she thought would be too small. Yet, she told us, "Amazingly, they fit me perfectly." She also declared, "I truly never dream about Grandmother Marcia. So just the fact that she showed up made the dream memorable."

To understand this dream we need to consider the symbolism of shoes, the origin and characteristics of the shoes in question, and the qualities and attributes of her grandmother. Taking all this into consideration, if this were my dream, I would feel that my grandmother made a very special visit to me to give me a magnificent gift—her shoes (symbols of her attributes as a gentle, kind, and loving mother). That they actually fit me when I thought they would be too small reassures me that I will not find motherhood confining and I have within me the qualities and abilities of a loving mother. I would feel very blessed by this dream.

Sometimes dreams might announce the pregnancy to a woman before she knows it in waking life. A young woman with no intention of getting pregnant might have an anxiety dream of "what-if" that alerts her to a situation that may need to be resolved. She might not feel ready or prepared to become a parent. Such a dream might be an invitation to her to give the whole question serious consideration, and if necessary, to begin mental, physical, and spiritual preparations.

Anyone can dream of having a new baby, even men and post-menopausal woman. In these dreams babies are symbols for new areas of self-expression, such as a project for which one is responsible or a concept to which one has given birth. The baby may represent a work of art—a painting or sculpture, creative writing, or original music. It is uniquely your own creation of which you can be proud. In later dreams, you might be caring for the child, feeding it and watching it grow. This has been true for me.

Over the years I have repeatedly dreamed of giving birth. Once it happened three times during the same dream. The experiences are usually positive. I remember hearing beautiful choral music while awaiting one birth and rejoicing greatly after another.

But all is not ideal in every dream. In one or more dreams I had a miscarriage. In another I forgot I had a baby and became alarmed when I remembered. In yet another

I Panic Because I've Forgotten to Feed the Baby

. . . Owen and I are looking at baby clothes in a store.
I spot what appears to be an unusual cap for a toddler.
Actually someone else is looking at it and is about to
buy it. I think it is very cute. I wish I had someone to
give it to. Then I remember that we do have a new baby
at home. We could get something like that for it. Why
not? Even though it's just a baby now, it'll grow to need
that size. Then I begin to panic. I have forgotten to feed
the baby its midday feeding. We must hurry home. . . .

Forgetting you have a baby that needs to be fed is alarming, but what if you dream you have injured or killed a child? Here is a powerful answer to this question that Wilda Tanner gives in *The Mystical, Magical, Marvelous World of Dreams*:

"You may—much to your great dismay—find the baby dead or dying and realize that you have sacrificed it in some way or dropped and killed it accidentally. This can be a very disturbing dream until you realize the baby represents your valued project, not a real child, and that the dream is suggesting that it may not be wise to 'let the matter drop' or to sacrifice your ideas or ideals for the sake of someone else (which is something we too often do to ourselves). The dream may point out that you have allowed another person to belittle your hopes and plans to the point of dropping them, or you have permitted them to talk you out of what you really wanted to do with your life or talents. In such a case, the dream would show you are sacrificing more than a baby—you are literally sacrificing a very dear and valued part of yourself, hence the highly significant symbolism of your 'baby.'"

I haven't had such an extreme dream of neglect, but six years prior to the dream above the following dream expressed similar circumstances of forgetting:

I Have a New Baby to Care For

> I have a new baby to care for. I don't remember many
> details. I evidently set the baby down somewhere or give
> it to someone to look after and go on about my business.
> Then at least once I become alarmed wondering where it
> is. I find it and it is okay.

If this were the dream of a young expectant mother, it would likely be dealing with her relationship with her unborn child, expressing her anxieties and concerns about whether she will be a good mother. But in this case, it was a dream I had at age 59. In this dream I remembered the baby and found it was okay. I evidently had put a project aside for a while. The dream was reminding me to stay with the project.

RACHEL G. NORMENT, M.A.

this child?" Owen had told me the following dream in which he and I are together:

Time Now for Baby Ethan

> The dream takes on a distinctively erotic mood. We are naked, standing, hugging, thinking of making love and we conclude that it is appropriate now to go ahead and start "*the* baby," whose name will be Ethan. I wake up then.

We can assume that the meaning will be symbolic; I was past the age for conceiving a child. Owen had no idea where the notion of that particular name came from; it just seemed to be announced as a fact in the dream. In Hebrew, "Ethan" means long-lived and is given to a child as a good omen. Since he would soon be fully retired from his teaching duties, perhaps these last two dreams were reminding Owen that he would be having more time for creative endeavors. He did feel the dream might signify a new possibility in his life.

I was the one who would be giving birth in this last dream. But sometimes men dream they are giving birth. David Lohff in *The Dream Dictionary* states a man who dreams this might be "in a situation where his virility or creative participation in the world is in question. This occurs most among men who see themselves as less creative than they would like to be. The dream serves as a form of compensation to illuminate the more creative facets of their personality. Men who are pregnant do not give birth exclusively to children, but a wide range of objects that somehow support their mission in the world."

I don't think Owen has ever dreamed he was the one giving birth, but I have dreamed at least twice that he was giving birth. The first time, in 1992:

Owen Is Going to Have a Baby

> Owen and I are going to a small old-fashioned-looking clinic or hospital. People are being checked by doctors. I don't remember the scene in detail except that it is decided that Owen is going to have a baby and he will have to stay

at this place while he waits during his pregnancy. The only space they have for him is in the corner of a large open room. There is a bed for him there. He doesn't like the fact that it is such a public place with no privacy, but he is accepting the fact that he needs to stay.

Giving birth can symbolize, simply, a new beginning. The night before I dreamed this, Owen told me he thought Jon Kabat-Zinn's *Full Catastrophe Living* would be the book that would save his life, or at least, keep him from having to take medication for high blood pressure. I was pleased to hear this. I felt this was signaling the beginning of a new phase of his life. He was in a state of anticipatory pregnancy.

In another one, in 1999:

Owen Gives Birth to a Manufactured Baby

Owen is with me in an unidentified place. He is acting upset about something. I don't know what. At one point he stretches out crosswise between two beds, partially on the bed. . . . But before I see what actually takes place he lifts what appears to be a fully developed newborn infant from near him and places it on a pillow. Then he stretches out on the bed. While doing this he is moaning and calling out: "Now look what we have done. I've had a baby." He is despairing and implying we have done something desperately wrong and the result is that he has given birth to a baby. I go to it, pick it up, and examine it. I become aware that it is not a real, live baby. There are some markings on its back that have a manufacturer's name on it. I tell Owen of this, that it's not really a baby.

Obviously, this dream cannot be considered to be literal. Owen, in the dream, probably represented my animus, the masculine attributes within me that produced some new creation—the baby in the dream. But it was not a real baby; it was "manufactured." What could this mean? Perhaps this new creation was contrived and artificial and did not really emerge from or represent my true self. Had I produced something that did not represent my true self? Another possibility: Did Owen represent himself in my dream? Was my dreammaker pointing out to me that I felt something my husband had created at that time was not representative of his true self?

I confess I did not try to fully understand this dream back in 1999 when I had it. But since it has caught my eye while reviewing my dreams, its significance can still be important. We both probably would benefit from questioning the "authenticity" of our "creations" at that time.

If you dream of having a baby, there is probably something new in your life that needs great care and attention, as does a baby. Recognize and accept this responsibility with mindfulness and joy.

The Magical/Divine Child

Sometimes the babies in our dreams grow and mature much more rapidly than a normal baby. I have had several in which this was the case. I found them interesting, but did not understand them to begin with. Let's look at several of these.

I'm Given the Responsibility of Looking After a Very Rapidly Growing Baby

> A tiny, almost newborn baby needs to be taken care of.
> I don't know its origin, but in the dream it is not my
> own birth baby. But it is taken into our home and grows
> rapidly. At only two or three months it is almost as large
> as a year-old child. I'm having to watch it closely I
> need to go off with someone, maybe to do errands. I try
> to find a sitter to look after the baby while I'm gone to
> keep it safe and out of trouble.

Almost two and a half years later:

The Four Month Old Baby Can Walk and Talk

> I dream I am holding a baby on my lap while visiting at
> a friend's house.

I ask how old the baby is. I'm told four months. Later when the baby is placed in a playpen I'm amazed to see it pull itself up and walk around the pen. At another point I ask again, "How old did you say, four months?" I'm startled when the *baby* replies, "Yes, Ma'am."

Then after a three-year interval I dreamed:

I'm Alarmed When Someone Steals My Beautiful, Precociously Developed Baby Girl

I have recently given birth to a baby girl. While caring for her I become aware that she seems to be developing very rapidly—both mentally and physically. Although she is still relatively newborn, when I talk to her I see in her eyes that she understands what I am saying to her. I talk to her as I would a much older child—perhaps even a young adult—and I know she comprehends everything. I am struck by the beauty of this child. Her physical growth accelerates much beyond normal. . . . While still needing diapers and before any baby normally would be doing so, she is walking around with the ease of an older child, wanting to run and play with other children. She looks as if she is four or five years old. . . . I am alarmed to see some adult take her by the hand and lead her away. I immediately give chase. . . .

It was about this time that I read *Crossing to Avalon* by Jean Shinoda Bolen and took note of the following passage: "The magical child archetype appears in the dreams of people who are getting in touch with meaning or creativity in their lives and sense that they might have a personal destiny to fulfill. . . . Characteristically this is a dream that arises in conjunction with a new connection with the archetype of the Self, the archetype through which we derive a sense of meaning and affiliation with something greater than our small selves. The dream appears with the possibility of new or renewed life. The soul is awakening."

We Take In an Orphaned Boy

(2) Quite suddenly and unexpectedly we learn of a very young, orphaned boy whom we decide we should take into our household and probably adopt. . . .

I Lovingly Care for Girls We Plan to Adopt

(3) My husband and I have taken in two young girls, evidently orphans. I'm not sure of their exact ages, maybe six to eight or nine. I interact with them very lovingly. We are considering adopting them. After having them for a while, my husband and I decide we *will* adopt. . . .

In each dream, my dream ego had taken into our household an orphaned child and intended to care for it, even adopt it. This could represent becoming aware of some part of myself that was abandoned and deciding to take it in, accept it, and adopt it (incorporate it into my psyche). I had recovered some neglected aspect of myself. This was a very positive undertaking. Young boys in the dreams might represent what is often considered the masculine attributes of doing and thinking; the girls the feminine attributes of feeling and being. In our American culture in the past century most people valued the masculine characteristics more than the feminine. Were these first two dreams bringing into my awareness the possibility that I thought I didn't possess the admired masculine attributes? The dreams were showing me I had them.

The age of the child in the dream is important. The child might be a symbol for the dreamer at that age. What was happening then probably has some bearing on the dreamer's current situation. I did not specify the exact age of these children; sometimes you don't recall such details when you record your dreams. I can try to remember my waking-life circumstances when I was these ages. Was I experiencing problems— physical or psychological—that had some bearing on my life at the time I had these dreams? Sometimes the age of the child relates to something in one's life that many years prior to the time of the dream. So if the child is eight years old in your dream, try to recall what was going on in your life when you were eight, or eight years prior to the time of the dream.

Since dreams speak to us on many levels, sometimes they may be helping with situations involving our waking-life children. If your child is identified by name in the dream, see if the dream events are connecting you with some current situation in your family. Even then, on a different level, your child can represent a part of yourself that has the same characteristics as your child.

All children need to be nurtured, to be allowed to develop to their full potential. Our dreams come to help guide us in doing just this, whether the dream child represents a part of ourselves, our waking-life children, or our creative ideas and new projects. We can be encouraged by dreams that show we are giving loving care and helpful guidance to young children. Dreams of children come to help us move in a life-expanding direction on our life's journey.

A Baptism Ritual Dream

Rituals are often special initiation rites signifying new beginnings at specific stages in our lives. Among the most common are baptism, school commencement ceremonies, and marriage ceremonies. Ancient cultures had many initiation ceremonies we no longer observe. Jean Dalby Clift and Wallace B. Clift lament this demise in their book *The Hero Journey in Dreams*. They say that as a result of this demise, "the psyche of individuals today often resorts to dream imagery. The dreams produce ritual imagery when the dreamer is ready to move from one status to another."

Through the years I have experienced many ceremonial or ritual dreams. Some were extremely strange, almost bizarre. Stephen Larsen notes in *The Mythic Imagination* that "the shocking quality of imagery [in some ritual dreams] is necessary to the symbolic rite of transformation." Such dreams can be very disturbing unless one realizes that these are metaphorical and symbolic. One of the most memorable of these was one that seemed to be a baptism of a baby. This dream occurred in December 1996:

I Observe a Ritual of Baptism

There has been a birth in the family. I'm not sure who the baby "belongs to." There is a special ceremony going on outside—a special cleansing and protective procedure on the newborn. A special physician is carefully cleansing the baby's body. Next the physician cuts a large circular segment of the baby's skull and lifts it off, places it aside, and then carefully swathes (cleans) around the inner surface of the head. Others and I are standing around witnessing this special procedure. We are amazed at what we see. We do not understand what is taking place, but we watch very intently. After this part is finished, the doctor places the skull piece back on top. I'm wondering if he'll sew it in place. I'm surprised when he just pushes the baby, who at this point evidently is in a vat of liquid, so it goes completely under the liquid. I'm startled, at first fearful for the baby's safety. Then I remember that babies can be submerged in water safely, if they don't stay under too long. When the baby comes up the head area is completely healed over—and the baby is fine. The doctor takes the baby and hands it to me. I lovingly take it into my arms. I'm delighted to be allowed to hold it. It looks into my eyes in such a way I feel we bond. After a bit I look around to find someone to hand the baby to next. I'm not sure who this is—probably the young mother.

This dream was discussed several months later at a dream workshop conducted by psychotherapist Barry Williams during a *Journey into Wholeness* Conference at St. Simons Island, Georgia. Williams felt this was a perfect example of a ritual dream.

Baptism is a symbol of purification, a cleansing. Since each person within a dream may represent a part of the dreamer, an inner healer within me was performing this amazing and startling procedure. The physician cleansed the baby's body, then "cuts a large circular segment of the baby's skull and lifts it off, places it aside, and then carefully swathes (cleans) around the inner surface of the head."

Williams explained that, symbolically, when the crown of the head is taken off, you expose its vulnerability to higher (positive) energies. The cleaning of the inner surface of the head might suggest a clearing away of old ideas, thoughts, and attitudes.

Instead of sewing the skull back on, after replacing the top of the skull the physician pushed the baby completely under the water. Surprisingly, when the baby reemerged, the head appeared to be completely healed, made whole again. Immersion in water is frequently part of a baptismal ceremony. It can represent the washing away of the old state of being and a return to the original state of wholeness and purity prior to birth; it is a form of healing.

Baptism also symbolizes a new beginning and is often a dedication to a spiritual life. Four and a half years earlier I had a different dream, which I will discuss in Chapter 22, that told of my commitment to a spiritual "service"—my vocation. Perhaps this dream of baptism was announcing that it was time to begin this service. This dream has a double image of a new beginning since a baby, also, is a symbol for new life. A new baby, a new life, a new undertaking needs to be nurtured and cared for. Although in the dream I was not the mother, the baby's mother represented the nurturing part of myself that needed to nurture this new life. I did bond to the child when I looked into its eyes.

Barry Williams asked if anything "new" was going on in my life. When I told of various transitions—a new house in a new location, my husband's retirement, and life after recovering from cancer—he thought this dream was speaking positively of all this.

When I look back on this dream now and reflect on what it meant, and still means, I can see it indeed signaled the beginning of a very important new phase of my life. A study of many other dreams coming before and after this one revealed that I had been following a plan, unconsciously, preparing me for a new vocation. Aided by life experiences—even some they were unwanted at the time—I gradually have come to know my calling and then have consciously taken further preparatory steps.

This inner healer, personified as the physician in my ritual dream, is always there for me. He probably contributed greatly to my positive healing experiences during cancer treatments. Everyone has their own inner healer they can call upon. Part of my mission may be to help other people recognize this healing aspect within themselves. I can do this through teaching the importance of understanding and working with dreams. This healer works on many levels, physical, mental, psychological, and spiritual, helping one become the whole person one was meant to become.

—18—

CREATING A BOOK

The manifestation of any form of creativity takes time. In many of my dreams this was illustrated with the metaphor of pregnancy and giving birth. I dreamed the next three dreams while I was working on my first book, *Guided by Dreams*. The first one combines two relevant themes—taking tests and being pregnant:

Preparing for and Taking a Test in a Craft Class While Being Very Pregnant

> I am trying hard to learn all the material so I'll do well.
> I am also very pregnant. . . . I wonder if I'll get through
> the class and test before the baby comes. I do take the
> test in the dream.

This dream pointed out how hard I was working—learning all I could about dreams and creative writing in preparation for creating my first book. Once the creative project was underway, I dreamed:

I Await the Full Development of My Baby Before Its Birth

> It appears I'm pregnant and awaiting the birth. . . . (An
> acquaintance) is impatient for the birth to take place. I
> feel I need to be left alone to await the full development
> of the baby. It will come in its own good time.

image is similar to that of a baby beginning to push to be born, but the head appears more that of a much older person than a baby. I wonder at what I'm seeing. There doesn't seem to be space in the container for a body with this head. There's nothing I'm supposed to do to help it out; I'm just supposed to check on its progress. Again I leave it and close the lid. Quite some time later I remember I'm supposed to keep checking. Since it has been quite a long time since I last checked, I become alarmed. I wonder if I've waited too long and it has died because of my negligence.

What first struck me about this dream was the image of something making an effort to move upward. Perhaps this was material from the unconscious coming into consciousness. On one level I feel sure this applies. My dreams had been bringing lots of information into consciousness. But I felt it also dealt specifically with the book and its completion, when it would see the light of day, when it would be born. Many earlier dreams used the imagery of being pregnant and giving birth in reference to the creation of the book. This dream said that for the contents of the container to come out "it will need to push its way through a covering at the top that has begun to split open. I see what appears to be the top of a head. The image is similar to that of a baby beginning to push to be born." So the time of birth was almost here.

The puzzle was that there didn't appear to be space for more than a head in the container. The head is where we process and keep our thoughts; my memories and creative thoughts are what are written down in the book. I had been given the responsibility of caring for the contents of the container for quite some time, even before I knew what was there. The container's round (cylindrical) shape suggested the idea of a *temenos*, which in ancient Greece was thought to be a sacred place where one could find refuge and be safe from harm. This seems appropriate here in my dream. Whatever was in the container was being kept safe until the proper time for it to emerge. I was supposed to keep check on its progress and, I assume, let it out when the time was right. At the end of the dream I was alarmed, hoping my negligence hadn't caused its death. The answer to that concern was not revealed.

The appearance of just a head caught my attention for another reason. I remembered having dreamed of babies with just heads many years ago. At the time I speculated that the dream was saying that my head was separated from my body— perhaps I was too much in my head. On seeing this new dream, I decided to search for the old one to see how the two might be connected. In the process I discovered two additional dreams. One came in July of 1991, almost eight months before the remembered dream of babies with just heads. I believe the head in this one was an adult, not an infant.

A Head to Care For

> In an unidentified place, I am meeting some people,
> strangers that I don't know anything about, and I am
> asked to go over and care for one particular person,
> to look after him. When I go there I discover that the
> person is just a head. There is no body whatsoever.
> This doesn't seem to be particularly strange to me in
> the dream. I simply pick up the head and am going
> to do the caring for it, looking after it. The other
> circumstances of the dream have escaped me, but that
> does not seem to matter.

Since all characters in a dream can be considered parts of the dreamer, the people I was meeting were strangers, parts of myself I did not know. I was meeting and getting to know new parts of myself. Then I was asked to "go over and care for one particular person, to look after him." This "person" was just a head. On reflection, this seemed very strange, but in the dream it "doesn't seem to be particularly strange." The question again might be whether the dream was saying my head was disconnected from my body. For two reasons I don't believe that was its message. One, the head was only one part of the group of strangers I was meeting. There were many aspects of myself present. Then I was being asked to take special care of this "head." There didn't seem to be any criticism or negative connotation involved.

Now I find it amazing to realize I was being asked by my inner being, my dreammaker, my inner Self, to take special care of "the head" over a

During the time I was negotiating with a publisher, after I had completed the final draft of the book, I had this dream:

I Live in a Basement While I Wait

> I have my "wares"—what I have created—on display in
> a major hallway by the front door of a public building.
> This arrangement seems to be an ongoing matter. At
> some point I decide to move to an area farther down
> the hallway. There is a door leading off the area, maybe
> going to a basement. This space becomes my living
> space as well as a business space. There are other people,
> mainly women, living there. I may not be pleased
> to have to share the space, but I have to accept this.
> Someone tries to console me by saying that next spring I
> can move back by the front door, when it's warmer.

> This dream suggested disappointment in having to wait
> for my "wares"—maybe my book—to be prominently
> displayed (published). This makes sense. I felt it was
> taking a long time to get through the process of editing
> and I was very eager for the book to be published. In
> the meantime I took up residence deeper inside the
> building where there was a doorway leading into a
> basement (a symbol for one's unconscious). I would
> continue to live and conduct business there (study and
> write about dreams—messages from our inner selves)
> until warmer weather. Soon after having this dream, I
> signed a contract with a projected book release date of
> the following April or May.

When I was making a public announcement about the publication of the book, soon after I had the finished product in hand, I stated it this way: "I am 72 years old. I have just given birth. The gestation period lasted over 12 years. Labor lasted more than four years. But the delivery has finally taken place."

—19—

HEALING THROUGH DREAMWORK

There is a powerful healing potential within our dreams if we are willing to take notice and listen to their wisdom. The word for "dream" in Hebrew is *chalom* and is derived from the verb meaning "to be made healthy or strong." When we use the term "healing" do we mean getting rid of a physical illness?

Often we use the term "healing" broadly, to signify the actual "curing" of the physical or psychological illness. At times this is correct. But we need to bear in mind that "healing" does not always intend or include medical curing as such. Someone may be "healed" even when not "cured." This statement is based on the distinction between the meanings of the two words. The verb "to heal" is etymologically related to the Old English *hal* (whole); thus to heal, to restore to health, is to make whole. "To cure" is more accurately used as a medical term meaning "to get rid of a physical illness." Healing can take place even when a cure is not possible. Therefore terminally ill patients may have healing dreams that help them understand and peacefully accept their situations. Healing dreams of the dying can provide a "bridge" to help them feel comfortable in their transition to a new realm.

Kellogg's Categories of Healing Dreams

Ed Kellogg, Ph.D. in biochemistry from Duke University, a proficient lucid dreamer, has a long-standing interest in the phenomenology of dreaming. As part of an online PsiberDreaming Conference of the International Association for the Study of Dreams he presented a paper and workshop that looked at three kinds of healing dreams: *diagnostic, prescriptive,* and *curative.*

Diagnostic dreams point to a developing situation in the body, something that has already begun or something that might develop in the future, sometimes years before the person has any outward physical signs of disease. The mind-body connection within us is so strong that long before we become conscious of them our sleeping mind senses imbalances, then brings the situation into our consciousness through dreams.

These dreams can be literal or metaphorical. In a metaphorical dream, one's car or house may have a problem. The car or house can represent the dreamer's body; therefore its problem refers to something wrong with his or her body. If one has been working with dreams and is aware of his/her personal symbols, one might understand the dream well enough to seek help from a physician in time to prevent a full-fledged illness or forestall serious complications. In a literal dream a woman may dream of finding a lump in her breast, which leads her to contact her doctor.

Prescriptive dreams can suggest a form of medical treatment for an illness or beneficial diets and health practices for the dreamer. If foods are mentioned in a positive context, the particular food is likely to be beneficial if included in one's diet. If presented in a negative context, the food might best be avoided.

According to Kellogg, people experiencing *curative dreams* are healed "directly, through a mind-body-spirit integration effect, partially or completely. However, in most cases a curative healing dream only begins a process that will take time to complete." I believe Kellogg, here, is overlapping the term "healing" with "curing."

Some people awaken healed (cured) or much improved following a healing dream. This is reminiscent of "healings" experienced centuries ago by people in ancient Greece who visited the temple of Aesclepius, where they might receive information in a dream to aid healing or even be healed directly.

Kellogg reminds us that dreams may belong to one, two, or all three of these categories. "For example diagnostic healing dreams may also show the cause of a developing condition, which if eliminated might well halt or reverse the dis-ease process." It is up to the dreamer to make the choice to do what is best after considering all the facts given by doctors and one's dreams.

A Prescriptive Dream

The potential message a dream brings is dependent upon the context, when and under what circumstances the dream comes. Let's see how this works with the following dream:

I Will Accept the Role of Doctor

> I'm attending a gathering where a serious discussion of
> the needs of the community is being held. It is decided
> that someone needs to be appointed to the role of
> "doctor." They begin considering who should be asked
> to accept this role. After some consideration some
> woman speaks up, turning to me asks, "How about you?
> Do you think you would consider doing this?"

If this were the dream of a young person who was considering what should be his/her life work, we might think the dream was asking, "Do you want to be a doctor?" But was it?

The dream continued:

> I respond that perhaps I would. I sense that some in
> the group are puzzled, perhaps amazed, that I would
> consider myself able to do this. As I'm speaking, possible
> ideas begin to form in my mind. I think to myself that
> my Reiki (a kind of "hands-on healing") ability is a form
> of administering healing. I almost say this out loud,
> but then I decide it wiser not to. I also think I would
> be able to listen to the concerns of young teenage girls
> and perhaps could inspire them in various ways. I look
> around at several standing nearby and I begin to hum a
> tune with a "catchy" rhythm. First one and then another
> of the girls begins to join in the singing and to let their
> bodies sway in time to the tune. I spontaneously decide
> to lead them in a dance line, and motion for them to
> follow me. Gradually the whole group joins in and I

lead a dancing line around an adjoining field. I think
to myself that this kind of activity is "healing" and
would be beneficial as a form of exercise. It would be
good for me to encourage this by example and my own
enthusiasm. This will inspire without their even being
aware of what it is doing for them. They will consider it
a fun activity that they enjoy doing. I ponder to myself
whom I would be able to help this way. I answer my
own question with the words "inner city people who do
not have access to help."

In one way this sounds like a person wanting to help the needy by becoming
an "inner city" doctor. But this was a dream I had at age 65, five years after
going through my cancer experience. So what could this mean?

I had already trained in the healing practice of Reiki. So one might
think I was considering putting this ability to use more publicly than I had
previously. But the dream stated I decided it "wiser not to... say this out
loud." This was not my intention both in the dream and in waking life.

Since in one approach to dreamwork everything in a dream represents
a part of oneself, a "community" could be everything that makes up the
dreamer, all aspects of the person—thus my personality, health, abilities,
fears, anxieties, hopes, etc. The phrase "inner city people" supports this
idea, perhaps meaning my inner parts—physical, mental and spiritual.

I believe I was acknowledging to a part of myself that I can be my
own healing force. Other parts may wonder whether this is possible. I can
use my Reiki healing ability on myself. I can do various things to inspire
and encourage the still young parts of myself. To promote continued good
health, I realize I need exercise. Many forms of exercise have never appealed
to me, even when I was young. But singing and dancing to beautiful music
have always been fun. If I would do this, it would be very beneficial and
healing.

The dream was suggesting a positive means for me to promote my
own "wholeness," physical, mental, and spiritual health. I need to keep
reminding myself of this.

So far I have concentrated my thoughts about this dream on what it
says I can do for myself. But it might also be referring to what I am being

called to do for others. As I have been explaining throughout this book, dreamwork can be healing on multiple levels. Thus, you might say, in one sense anyone who helps someone understand his or her dreams has the role of a "doctor" who helps one "heal." The dream was not calling me to be a medical doctor, but to be a healer in this sense.

Dream Guidance Towards Healing

Dreams can give a forewarning about a body ailment, sometimes years before the person has any outward physical signs of disease. If you have been working with dreams and are aware of your personal symbols, you might understand the dream well enough to seek help from a physician in time to prevent a full-fledged illness or forestall serious complications. I wish I had known more about dream interpretation in 1992 when I had the following dream:

My Kitten's Strange Growth Needs to Be Cut Off

> I have a pet cat that I love. I discover it has a branching (shrub-like) growth coming out of its body's underside. I find the kitten crouched under a sideboard. I pick it up so I can cut off this growth. I hold it and caress it lovingly.

At the time I didn't understand the symbolism of this dream. Two years later I was diagnosed with breast cancer. When I looked back on this dream years later, now understanding that a kitten in my dreams frequently is a symbol for myself, I wondered if it could have helped to have understood the message sooner.

Five months after having the above dream and still over a year before my diagnosis, I had a dream describing a form of biopsy I would undergo I had not heard of before experiencing it. In the dream I was given

Medical Tests with a Tube Inserted

> Others and I are undergoing some kind of "tests" that seem to be medical. We are being anesthetized to have

a "tube" or something inserted. This will be left in our
bodies so the results can be observed and recorded.

This is the kind of dream you are tempted not to record because you
remember so little and you can't see its significance. Since I had never
heard of a needle localization biopsy, I had no idea what this dream was
referring to.

By the time I received my diagnosis I had studied dreams enough to
know I might be able to receive beneficial guidance from any forthcoming
dreams. On the third morning after receiving the diagnosis I remembered
a series of six dreams. This is the "initial dream series" I referred to in
Chapter 6. In them I was attending some kind of educational conference.
The various "scenes" seemed somehow connected.

The first dream illustrated metaphorically my precarious situation and
my reaction to it. I believed the second dream was very significant to the
present time; I hoped it might help answer the question uppermost in my
mind: Who should perform the lumpectomy?

In the dream,

The Short Man Easily and Gently Carries Me

I am with two men. One is thin and shorter than the
other. He looks at me very kindly and somehow I know
he wants to pick me up and carry me. I say I think I
am much too big and heavy for him. The other man is
bigger, taller. He is just standing there doing and saying
nothing. I don't know the men; I don't know their
names. The shorter man responds that he can lift me:
"We'll see what I can do." He very slowly and gently
eases me up so I am horizontal and am being held close
to him . . . . He then slowly and gently eases and turns
me around, moving me several feet farther over in the
room or space where we are . . . . I am amazed at the
ease and gentleness with which he does this.

I felt this dream was suggesting who should do the lumpectomy, but for a long time I wasn't sure what the suggestion was. After engaging in lengthy consultations with several doctors including a radiation oncologist, I became convinced the gentle, shorter man in the dream was the radiation oncologist who could carry me further along my treatments after the original surgeon had completed his part. I chose this route for my treatments and came through the whole experience remarkably well.

After I completed my radiation treatments I wrote to this doctor, telling him the story of how I chose him. I expressed gratitude for the excellent care he and his staff provided and for being guided into making choices that proved to be right for me. Something very amazing was going on with the dream. A few days later I received this reply from him: "Thank you for sharing your thoughts with me. I was very touched by this little essay. It makes one wonder whether there are forces that we don't understand that are at work, guiding us in one direction or another."

Many months—even years—later, after studying these dreams further, I realized that the other four dreams pointed to means of healing and showed future events following my treatments. At the time I could see only what the dreams were saying on an external, and at times literal, level. My mind was so caught up with the immediate medical experience and my working knowledge of dream symbolism was so limited that I missed the deeper, inner symbolism. I forgot that all characters in a dream are at a deep level symbols for parts of oneself. Thus, the various men in this series of dreams could represent my inner masculine attributes and were available to help me through this experience.

My book *Guided by Dreams* gives a detailed account of my experiences, thoughts, and emotions surrounding my diagnosis and treatments for breast cancer and how I used knowledge gained through dream interpretation to make decisions during the course of my treatment and in the years following.

More Examples of Dream Guidance

As we have already stated, some dreams do actually deal with physical ailments and can warn of oncoming health problems, diagnose ailments, suggest treatment, and accelerate the healing process. They can be both literal and metaphorical.

In his book *Healing Dreams* Marc Barasch discusses how his own dreams and those of others led to healing. In his own case, after experiencing a series of vivid, mysterious and disturbing dreams, he was jolted to attention by a metaphorical dream. In this dream, torturers hung a pot filled with hot coals under his chin. He reports, "I woke up screaming, the odor of searing flesh in my nostrils—I couldn't ignore them any longer. I was sure that something inside me had gone drastically wrong. Each successive dream had spelled it out more explicitly until, although the word was never uttered, it glared down at me from a neon marquee: cancer."

Although he immediately went to his doctor, it took persistence after more nightmares before the skeptical doctor ordered a needle biopsy. Barasch had to overcome his own fears before he allowed a biopsy, which revealed a malignant tumor of the thyroid gland, and later the surgical removal of the cancer.

Wanda Burch, in her book *She Who Dreams,* describes both metaphorical and literal dreams that foretold of her breast cancer. Even though she intuitively "knew" she had cancer, she hoped the dreams were warning of some other problem in her life. Doctors were reluctant to believe she was not imagining a problem.

Later, before she finally received the diagnosis of breast cancer, she had a dream in which her deceased father named her disease. "He tells me, almost shouting, that I have a malignant lump in my breast and that I must have my breast removed." She had other dreams that told her of the exact location of the cancer.

Fortunately, once Burch received her diagnosis, her surgeon and oncologist were willing to listen to her dreams and they modeled treatments on the dreams she shared with them. She reports, "Together we stepped beyond science and discovered the right combination of medicine for the body and medicine for the mind."

Garfield's Seven Stages of Recovery

Psychologist, international authority on dreams, and one of the cofounders of the Association for the Study of Dreams, Patricia Garfield has written

The Healing Power of Dreams. From her own dreams and those of other people, she gives examples and explains how to actively participate in your own healing. Dreams can warn one of oncoming health problems, suggest treatment, and accelerate the healing process.

Garfield describes her experience following a fall in which her wrist was seriously injured. After misdiagnosing the seriousness of the injury, her orthopedist prescribed incorrect treatments. Ten days after the injury she dreamed that her arm was broken, returned to the doctor, and insisted on additional x-rays, which showed a complex fracture requiring surgery and extensive therapy. Garfield goes on to show how "each phase of sickness and returning wellness is traced in our dream imagery."

According to Garfield, there are seven stages of recovery from physical trauma, and "our dream metaphors about our bodies constantly change throughout the course of recovery." What follows is my brief summary of her very thorough discussion of how to explore and understand the body metaphors in our dreams.

The first stage is *Forewarning Dreams*, which seem to predict illness. The ancient Greeks called these "prodromal," meaning "running before." Symptoms of illness often show up in our dreams in metaphorical language before we are aware of any in waking life. They are "probably responses of the brain to minute bodily sensations that are magnified and dramatized during sleep." Kellogg includes *Forewarning Dreams* under his category of *Diagnostic Dreams.*

Garfield's dream of her arm being broken is an example of her second stage: *Diagnostic Dreams.* Her dreammaker seemed to sift through various puzzling symptoms to come up with a diagnosis. If you can train yourself to find danger signs in your dreams, you will be able to seek early treatment, thus speeding recovery.

Stage 3 *Crisis Dreams* come when we have been seriously injured, have developed a disease, or are facing surgery. These dreams contain catastrophic images that symbolically show our fear of destruction and perhaps a fear of being surgically cut. Surgery might be depicted "as an invasion by knife or bullet or phallus, by wild animal or warrior." Other images may show the location and sensations of disturbed body parts. A few hopeful images may appear. Being able to recognize these positive images can be very helpful. Then various activities, such as drawing these images or using them in visualizations, can help accelerate the recovery process.

During the actual crisis we are likely to sleep poorly and not remember many dreams. Some medicines suppress dreaming. As medication is reduced, the brain may try to compensate for its dream inhibition and restore its normal functioning by experiencing "REM rebound," a state of terrifying dreams. These are Stage 4 *Post-Crisis Dreams*. This stage also includes post-traumatic stress dreams. The intensity of such nightmares and how long they will continue depend upon the degree of bodily damage undergone and the circumstances under which it was inflicted.

In Stage 5 *Healing Dreams*, as we return to health, new elements begin to appear in our dreams, often images of "new" things (newborn animals or babies, new clothing, new or restored houses) that are metaphors for an evolving new body image. Other images may depict a sense of recovering control over one's life, regaining energy, and feeling supported and loved. There have been reported cases in which people have been healed within the dream state. They dreamed of the recovery of a damaged body part, then awakened to find it true: a paralysis or migraine headaches had vanished, an arthritic condition had improved.

In Stage 6 *Convalescence Dreams*, which occur in the latter stage of healing, more normal dreams begin to appear. Dreams portraying accidents or operations become infrequent, and nightmares rare. Dreams of the healing phase are more frequent. Pay special attention to the "[d]reams that dramatize optimistic thought about a restored body. . . . [D]rawing these images and using them in visualizations help encourage the healing they represent."

When we have regained our health, we experience Stage 7 *Wellness Dreams*, dreams with images showing "the dreamer functioning normally and with assurance," as well as typical topics of the ups and downs of everyday life.

Garfield points out, "Our dream metaphors about our bodies change throughout the course of" an illness. In forewarning dreams symptoms of illness often show up in metaphorical language using universal symbols that might point to imbalances or illnesses. Something wrong with cars, houses, and even animals, representing our bodies, suggest problems. Forewarning dreams can also be diagnostic dreams. Sometimes they can point to the location and sensations of disturbed body parts. As we return to health, new elements—positive, hopeful images—may show up in our dreams. Garfield recommends "drawing these images or using them in visualizations" to help accelerate the recovery process. One does not need to be an artist; simple doodles and rough drawings are beneficial. Images of "new" things—newborn animals or babies, new clothing, new or restored houses—are metaphors for an evolving new body image. Other images may depict a sense of recovering control over one's life, regaining energy, and feeling supported and loved.

An Author's Account of a Healing Dream

How can dreams be agents for healing? The experiences of Marc Barasch and Wanda Burch show us how. We are given another inspiring example by L. Robert Keck in his book *Healing As A Sacred Path: A Story of Personal, Medical, and Spiritual Transformation.*

In midlife, after years of what he describes as "a descent into hell–polio, broken back, excessively severe chronic pain, and crippling," Keck had a healing dream. It did not "speak to healing directly. It spoke of wholeness, and it spoke of [his] untapped potential, the previously unknown portion of [his] being." He calls it his "Architect Dream."

To understand the importance of this dream, we need to know what led up to it. Multiple, wrenchingly painful illnesses during his high school and college years challenged his self-image as an athlete and his hopes of a career as a professional athlete. After intense and painful therapy he gained physical rehabilitation, making possible the opportunity to see a fulfillment of his dreams. He was offered contracts to play professional football and baseball. However, while mulling over these offers he had a life-changing inner experience, which led him into the professional ministry after obtaining a graduate degree in theology.

Years later he experienced a return of polio in the form of "post-polio syndrome." Doctors predicted a steady increase in symptoms including severe pain and permanent confinement to a wheelchair. Also, after many years of marriage and individual counseling, he and his wife realized their differences were irreconcilable and started divorce proceedings. He felt his sense of his soul-self was being wiped out. While experiencing deep despair over his life situation, he had his healing dream, which accurately predicted the subsequent thirty years.

In his dream, he heard voices in his basement. Upon investigation he discovered an architect's office there. The architect explained to Keck that he had designed his home and that there were many rooms in the house of which he was not aware before. Then the architect gave him a tour of the house, showing him the many rooms that he had not known existed. Keck states: "When the dream concluded, I was so changed by what the architect had shown me, in this much larger and much more wonderful home, that I decided not to go back to my former job, but begin giving tours of the house. . . . Although it was a long and gradual process of awakening for me, my Architect Dream was a powerful symbol of the sacred path that I was to take on my way into a miracle healing."

This dream is a typical, archetypal dream of healing. Many dreamers have had one like it; many will have such in the future. In a dream with this theme we learn that there are many more possibilities for our lives than we are aware; the unknown rooms in our houses represent these possibilities and aspects of our lives that can be explored and inhabited.

Keck considers this dream to be a wake-up call from God, which pointed out "how my constricted and restricted notions of human potential were blocking me from the healing I so desperately needed and wanted." The dream predicted a process that would lead to a miraculous healing and a change in the direction and content of his life and ministry. However, it took him a while to realize this. As many of us do, he wrote the dream down the next morning, and then forgot about it for several months. However, he did have a profound hope that he could be healed. He began to explore the previously "unknown rooms in his house." He read everything he could find on extended human potential and experimented with many of the newly emerging (in the 1970s) mind-body-spirit modalities; in particular, stress management through biofeedback, hypnosis, and meditative disciplines.

Keck gradually came to the significant realization that each person is unique in important respects. He states: "We will never know our full potential for health promotion, disease prevention, and participating in healing processes until we explore that uniqueness completely and thoroughly."

Keck gives data pointing to the gradual evolution in the medical profession towards acceptance of a more holistic approach to healing.

He also points out a need for a "powerful synergy between an evolving medicine and an evolving spirituality." He urges religious scholars and spiritual practitioners to become trained in integrating spirituality and healing, in order to bring the needed balance to this synergy, "wherein the whole of our knowledge and practice in health and illness will be more than the sum of the individual parts."

The Mind-Body Connection

How is it that dreams can show us things we are not aware of in waking life? The mind-body connection within us is so strong that our sleeping mind, our inner self, senses imbalances long before we become conscious of them. Sometimes we may have a vague awareness, but we don't want to face what this awareness might suggest. Our dreams come to make us aware of problems so we can do something about them. Frightening nightmares say, "Wake up! Pay attention! There is something very important you need to do for the sake of your health and wholeness."

Candace Pert, Ph.D., a biophysics and physiology researcher, made discoveries in the 1980s that confirmed an intricate biochemical communication network between the body and mind. Since emotions play a major role in the mind/body phenomenon, Pert emphasized that for maximum functioning of the immune system it is important to free blocked emotions and find constructive ways to express them. Dreamwork is a way to do this. It is a complementary therapy that has been overlooked for too long. We all need to become aware of the important role our dreams, agents of our inner healers, can play in our healing journeys.

Wendy Pannier and Tallulah Lyons, members of IASD and co-founders of the Healing Power of Dreams Cancer Project, now called the IASD Health Care Project, for more than a decade have used dreamwork with cancer patients at Cancer Support Communities in Philadelphia and Atlanta. They report: "We have seen how powerful dream imagery can be. We believe our work with dream imagery has application for other types of illness too—and for anyone seeking a fuller sense of wellness in life. We use the recognized and proven modality of guided imagery techniques and take them to the next level by customizing them with the individual's own dream imagery. This work falls into two primary categories: Transforming negative dream images (such as those from nightmares) and reinforcing positive and healing dream images by using them with imagery work in combination with other integrative medicine modalities."

A survey of their dream group participants found the following: Dreamwork brings about

(1) decreased feelings of anxiety and stress.

(2) an increased sense of connection with others.

(3) an increased sense of connection to inner resources.

(4) an increased understanding of healing at multiple levels.

(5) an increased quality of life—particularly emotional, social and spiritual.

(6) increased feelings of control over life and health issues.

(7) increased feelings of hope.

(8) an understanding of how to live fully now, despite cancer.

"Healing," in the truest sense of the word, can take place even when a "cure" is not possible.

Since 2006, I have been working with Lyons and Pannier to introduce and encourage the use of dreamwork as a complementary therapy. Dreamwork is beneficial for everyone, but can be especially helpful for persons experiencing serious illness. The personal stories recounted above illustrate the value of including dreamwork into healing therapies. Although the "evolutionary process" has been slow, the value of incorporation of dreamwork into the field of complementary therapy is gradually being recognized by more and more healthcare therapists and health centers.

Tallulah Lyons' book *Dreams and Guided Imagery: Gifts for Transforming Illness and Crisis* provides the opportunity through which many people may understand the concept of healing through dreamwork and learn how this is done.

—20—

Travel in Dreams

Since our dreams use metaphors to describe and/or illuminate our life journeys, it seems only natural that we find many dreams depicting times we are traveling. These may tell of occasions as simple as a walk down the street or they may describe a major trip overseas. The means of travel, where we are going and with whom, if anyone, tell us much about what is going on in our lives. Are we driving our own vehicle or is someone else at the controls? Are we taking public transportation or are we walking? Are the roads open or blocked, rough or smooth?

Life as a Day's Journey

Since dreams often use symbols to represent ideas, a "day" might represent one's life span instead of an actual day. Dream characters might be literal representations of persons in our lives or they might represent various aspects of ourselves.

In January 1998 I dreamed

Owen Has to Take His Mother Home Before We Make Our Journey

> Owen and I are getting ready to take a trip. I am
> getting things together, making final preparations in
> the morning, expecting to leave soon. I'm somewhat
> surprised and disappointed to learn that our departure
> must be postponed while my husband takes his mother
> home. In the dream his mother does not look like or

have the same characteristics she had in waking life.
She looks thin, frail, sort of wimpish and ineffectual.
He plans to get her to her destination and then return
in time for us to begin our journey today. I have also
expected we would get to our destination today, but I
don't see how this will be possible now. . . . It is fairly
late afternoon when he returns. I'm wondering if we
should wait till tomorrow to begin our journey. He has
been assuming we will go ahead and go, and says it will
be all right for us to set out this late in the day.

If my husband and I had been planning a trip in waking life that needed
to be delayed in a manner similar to the dream, we might consider the
dream to be literal. But my husband's mother was already deceased when
the dream occurred. Then, too, the dream states that the dream mother
"does not look like or have same characteristics she had in waking life."
So the dream is not literal.

Let's consider the idea that a "day" might represent one's life span. The
morning hours of the day might represent the first part of one's life. In
this case and in the dream, my husband's mother was present during this
early time. The dream might be saying that the son must help his mother
during this time and come to an understanding of his life entanglements
with her—how they affected his whole life—during the first part of the
day (his life).

Sometimes we receive dream messages for someone else. The dream
could be referring to how my husband thinks of himself. Does he consider
himself to be unsuccessful and worthless? Did his life entanglements with
his mother contribute to these feelings? As suggested above, he might need
to come to an understanding of these entanglements and how they affected
his whole life before he can continue his life journey with me, before we
can set out on a new part of our life together. It is interesting to realize
that in the years since this dream in 1998 he has gained more conscious
awareness of himself psychologically, in large part due to his own work
with dreams.

Since I am the dreamer and the dream mother was "thin, frail, sort of
wimpish and ineffectual," I might question whether there is a part of me

that is like this dream mother. If so, it is undesirable and I would want to figure out how to change my ways. In reflection, I am aware that I have been conscious of this potential problem during most of our marriage and I have tried to guard against replicating any of her undesirable traits.

In the dream I was eager to begin our journey, to get on with a new phase of my life with my husband. I did not see how we could reach our destination the same day. Did I fear our lives would end (the day would end) before our hoped-for journey could be accomplished? As we age, we do become more conscious of our mortality. I feel that I have much more I hope to accomplish during this lifetime.

"It is fairly late afternoon when he returns." Thus, in the latter years of our lives he has fulfilled his duty to his mother, she (his mother) is "home," and perhaps he has a better understanding of himself. I was (in the dream) and am (now in waking life) delighted that my husband "says it will be all right for us to set out this late in the day." I was and am encouraged that he wants no further delay in getting on with our life adventures as planned.

Driving or Being Driven

Since dream language is symbolic and metaphorical, vehicles may represent how we travel down the road of life. Our lifestyle and economic circumstances might be revealed by the size and type of vehicle and whether we have our own means of transportation. In the following dream I did not have my own car and

I Don't Know Where the Driver Is Taking Me

> I am in a different city from where I live. I need to get home and I don't have transportation. I get a ride with someone. After we have been driving for some time I notice we're driving in strange territory. We're not on the highway. I ask where we are going. The driver stops at a back-woods-type home. He is very gruff and displeased that I have questioned what he is doing. He says he is stopping to get gasoline.

I'm Frantically Preparing for a Trip When It's Time to Leave

Owen and I are about to embark upon a major trip—
perhaps overseas by boat. I'm packing. . . . Time is fast
approaching when we must depart for the ship this same
day. . . . I hear other people announcing we need to be
at the dock in five minutes. I'm frantically trying to pull
things together. I'm running out of time. I'm still at it
when we should be there.

In the dream I was preparing for a trip overseas. Perhaps in waking life I
was preparing for some major new undertaking, very different from my
usual activities. I dreamed I was trying to get organized and ready to go,
but I was still not ready when I needed to be. How many times do we feel
unprepared in our lives? This anxiety is also expressed in another common
dream theme of being unprepared to take a test, as discussed in Chapter
15. When we have these dreams, we can ask ourselves what it is we feel
unprepared for and what can be done to get prepared.

I consider a trip across the ocean by boat to be a major voyage. Right
after I graduated from college, I made such a voyage when I went to Italy
with The Experiment in International Living. It was a marvelous, life-
enhancing experience—a trip/voyage of a lifetime. In a dream, an ocean
voyage might represent just that—the voyage of my life, the journey my
soul makes, my life's path.

To help you better understand a boat dream, note the size and kind of
ship and who is in command, whether the boat is in good condition, tied
up in one place or about to set sail, whether the voyage is being undertaken
for business or pleasure and the ride is smooth and peaceful or rough and
traumatic, and how you feel about the trip. The details of the dreams will
bring into consciousness issues that are influencing the course of your life's
journey. Through dream messages you may be given suggestions of ways
to make improvements and words of encouragement when you are headed
in the right direction.

Buses and trains provide means of group transportation along
predesignated routes. Dreams of traveling by these means might represent
going along with group thinking, preconceived ideas, not making your

own decisions, or not being true to your own beliefs and feelings. If you dream of missing the bus, you might assume you are missing opportunities to get where you want to go. But there might be a time when it is good to miss the bus.

At the end of a long, complicated dream in 2001 I was riding on a bus when I saw

The Bus Leaves Without the Girl

> . . . The bus makes a stop near a post office, just a few
> doors down the street. A young woman rushes off to put
> something in the mail. I know she is hoping to get right
> back on the bus before it moves on, but it leaves without her.

When we have something to mail, it is often something we have written. The young woman (who represented a psychological aspect of the dreamer, myself) missed getting back on the bus after mailing her ideas, her self-expressions, to someone else. My ego—the "I" in the dream—thought the young woman wanted to get back on the bus. But did she? She might have chosen not to. If this was the case, part of me decided not to go along with group thinking or preconceived notions. I had differentiated my needs from the requirements established or routes taken by others. I could continue my journey on foot, going my individual way.

A month before the above dream, I had this dream:

The Woman Tells Me She Doesn't Want to Take the Bus Ride

> I am walking somewhere with a woman friend. I'm
> thinking she might like to ride a bus around a "loop"
> within the neighborhood to see the sights. I know a bus
> will be stopping soon at a nearby bus stop. I'm thinking
> the bus stops at the near end of the block, so I head us
> in that direction. Then I see other people queuing up a
> little further down the block. By this time the woman
> tells me she really doesn't want to take the bus ride, so
> we turn back.

225

In the dream, again "I" (the ego) thought the friend would want to ride the bus. But the "friend" (who represented some aspect of myself) did not want to go with the crowd, to get on the bus for even a brief ride around the neighborhood. I suspect I did not act upon this reluctance in waking life during the month between this dream and the similar one a month later. The dreammaker within us will repeat an idea, give us repeated motifs and themes until we pay attention and act upon the information revealed in the dreams. So look for as many clues as possible about what is going on within yourself. Our dreams bring things into our consciousness we may have forgotten or repressed or have never been aware of. They come to help us along our life journeys.

During the time I was trying to figure out my life's purpose I had a dream in which

I Don't Know My Destination When I'm Put on a Bus

I am with Owen and we have flagged a bus to see if it will take me where I need to go. Owen has my ticket, which I haven't seen. I don't know the destination. The bus will take me. I get on and my husband goes back to his vehicle to return to wherever he needs to be. After getting on the bus I realize I need to know where I'm going so I'll be able to get off at the right place. I . . . call to Owen, asking where the ticket is for. I can't hear his reply. . . . so now I don't consciously know the destination.

On one level this dream suggested I didn't know where I was headed in my life; I hadn't even thought about my destination before getting on a public means of transportation, perhaps an indication I was depending on others to facilitate my journey. I also had depended upon my husband to set my goals. From another perspective, it might be pointing out something different. My husband might represent my own masculine attributes that have been guiding me and setting my goals. I might have had a general notion about the direction of my life, but just didn't know how the journey would end. I might have been choosing to do something in the public arena and thus was using the public means of transportation in the dream. Dreams don't always reveal the whole story on a particular night. Thus in this dream, as in my waking life, I didn't yet know where my journey would take me.

Incubate a Dream

When the dream story seems incomplete, when we don't receive information that we hope we might get, we can "incubate" a dream by asking for a dream for further guidance. To do this, form the request in your mind as you are going to sleep. Then write down what you can remember about a response first thing in the morning. Sometimes we have to repeat this several times before we receive a response. Or, we need simply to wait for our lives to evolve as they will. A person's development often is a gradual process requiring a steady accumulation of knowledge and experience.

In 1993 I dreamed of being on a trip in a foreign country with several other people.

We're Caught While Exploring Forbidden Territory

We are driving and find ourselves going down the left fork in a road. We realize we are in territory that is not open to tourists. We continue on, interested in seeing what is there. We realize after a while that top-secret things are happening here, maybe war experiments or whatever. We decide we should stay but remain unnoticed by the people doing all this. We want to watch, observe, and learn as much as we can without getting caught. Later we fear we might be about to be discovered and we feel we should leave. We are about to escape when we are discovered. We may have been able to get some of the secrets out beforehand.

I had not taken a trip abroad recently nor was I planning such a trip. Thus we can consider the dream metaphorically. Exploring the territory in a foreign country can symbolize exploring unfamiliar ways of thinking or doing things. My ego——the "I"——believed we were seeing, discovering "top-secret things." I need to consider what was happening in my life at the time of the dream that felt like this kind of experience. What previously hidden knowledge was I learning? As the dreamer, I was eager to learn all I could and to pass on at least some of the knowledge before I was stopped. However, I did not explore this dream at the time to figure out its meaning. Then 12 years later I had a very similar dream. This time

We Nervously Await the Required Inspection

> I am in a foreign place. . . . To get into the country we probably had to pass through a kind of inspection. To get back out, the inspection/scrutiny is probably much stricter. As we wait in line to leave, we are very nervous. We have a "ticket" or document in hand, which we hope will pass muster without causing a problem. We have hidden other items that we fear might cause us to be imprisoned.

My initial thoughts about this dream were that perhaps the "inspection" process for getting into the country represented an application process for some program of learning. The document in hand when leaving might represent a diploma or certificate of completion. The inspectors might represent an inherited inner authority with restrictive beliefs that would inhibit my personal development if they prevailed.

Recently when I reread these thoughts I had a sudden "aha." The respective dates of these last two dreams sank in. The first one occurred in March just a few months before I had the first mammogram that looked suspicious. At this time any knowledge of the fact that I had breast cancer might have been classified as "top secret"; I certainly didn't know anything about it. They couldn't tell with any certainty that there was a problem, so they had me wait and return in six months to check again. Once I was given the cancer diagnosis I searched for as much information as possible. During my treatments I kept a careful record of everything that happened, thinking that perhaps some day what I experienced and learned might help someone else.

In the second dream, the country referred to might be the land of published authors. The dream said, "To get into the country we had to pass through some kind of inspection." This could be referring to the process of submitting the manuscript to a publisher. I wonder if the "document in hand" might be my manuscript for my book about dreams and my breast cancer experience. I had this dream in September of 2005 while we were in the final stages of editing in preparation for publication of the book. We certainly were "nervous" as we waited for the process to be completed and we hoped it would "pass muster without causing a problem"; we were eager for the "certificate of completion" — the published book itself.

—21—

New Insights Through Dreams

Our dreams are one of our best means of gaining new insights about our lives. They do not come to tell us what we already know; they invite us to new understandings. Sometimes we even sense in the dreams that they are coming to bring us messages. Here is a dream in which Owen was anticipating a message:

Waiting at Our House for a Message

My wife and I are in what appears to be our current house and neighborhood. We seem to be awaiting some sort of important message, though in what form isn't clear. I am aware of a man hurrying across adjacent lots toward our house and wonder if he is coming as a messenger. I feel some heightened anticipation, but beyond that this dream fades away.

Owen was unsure of what the message might be and how it might be brought to him.

Since all characters in a dream can represent parts of oneself, Owen might assume that he can receive the message from within himself, but he may have to wait longer to receive the message. Sometimes dreams do not tell everything the dreamer wishes to know. Later dreams may give more information.

Eight or nine days later Owen had this dream:

Receiving an Inner Message in My Car

I am sitting in my parked car, almost as if I had
awakened in the car, on what appears to be the street
where we live or in a generally similar neighborhood.
The streets are crowded with parked cars, notably the
one leading up the hill to our street. It is a very bright,
beautiful, comfortably warm day. I wonder why there
are so many cars. Then I have an intense feeling of
receiving an inner message—not a "voice" as such, but
an awareness of being somehow told, emphatically, "You
must live fully, intensely, in the present," or something
to this effect. I feel ecstatic hearing or sensing this as I
sit there in the car.

Owen needed to think deeply about this message. What would such
instructions mean in his life? What could he do to "live fully, intensely,
in the present"? He could give consideration to his circumstances and
feelings. He could also continue to examine additional dreams that might
provide further illumination.

Six months later he received further instructions:

Walking, Just Keep Walking

I am walking over an unfamiliar landscape,
somewhat rolling, barren, rocky. I am conscious of
various concerns and worries, and seem generally to
be wondering how to manage, how to live. I sense
very strongly that I am being given the instruction,
almost audibly and repeatedly, to *walk*, just keep
walking, walking. . . , which I think can be interpreted
figuratively and literally.

How is this an important message? Simply stated: literally it says to walk. Owen acknowledged that for many years jogging was his main form of exercise other than gardening. But as he has gotten older and experienced some medical problems, he no longer feels up to jogging. Yet he knows he needs to continue some kind of exercise program. His dream stated he was walking in an "unfamiliar landscape." Since he had retired, the terrain ahead may have looked both rocky and barren. He was also "conscious of various concerns and worries." He had the strong feeling that he was being told to "keep *walking, walking.*" The literal interpretation suggests that his exercise should be walking. Some of the problems of one's life can be helped by means of the physical exercise of walking. It can promote good circulation, encourage weight loss, help alleviate depression, and become a practice of meditative walking.

Since dreams have more than one level of meaning, we need to look beyond the literal to find deeper meanings. If one feels overwhelmed by life, "wondering how to manage, how to live," the deeper, figurative instruction to "keep walking" can mean keep going, don't give up.

These three dreams all seem related. Perhaps the last two are messages that were anticipated in the first one. Some dreams are much more complicated and harder to understand. For instance this dream of Owen's:

Gentle Man Walks into Angry Crowd

I am with a small group of people, on the portico of
an official building (government? college?), observing
a large, angry, threatening crowd in the area below the
steps. The evident leader or official in our group prepares
to go down among the crowd to try to calm them and
dispel any trouble. He is slight of build, calm, gentle, and
seemingly unafraid. Everyone with him is sure that he
will be set upon, beaten, likely killed. It is near darkness.
He proceeds down the steps and into the crowd.

Owen had not actually experienced such a situation in his life. What might this dream be telling him? If it were my dream and if the calm, gentle man represents some aspect of myself, this could well be a powerful new insight for me—to realize that there is within me a "calm, gentle, . . . unafraid" potential capable of walking into a threatening situation. This could be very empowering. The new insights that these dreams are bringing Owen are coming from a place deep within him, his Inner Self.

Spanning two or more decades Owen had two dreams that seemed to be warning him he was becoming an alcoholic. The first one more than 25 years ago had no plot or narrative, but was simply his own startled and somewhat anguished statement to himself, "I am an alcoholic!" Although not an alcoholic, he was beginning to drink moderately but fairly consistently on a day-to-day basis. While discussing this he stated, "There is a history of alcohol abuse on one side of my family, and I think the dream represented a kind of warning of what could come to pass if I were not careful." Then more recently he had a similar dream, again without narrative content. In this one he heard inwardly a kind of command. He's not sure, in recall, whether he heard the words "Stop drinking" or an admonition of great caution lest he find himself drinking more and more until it is out of control and he becomes a true alcoholic. He says he appreciates this dream: "This dream especially I take as a positive gift of warning, from my higher self or perhaps a spirit-connection, which I take very seriously and for which I am very grateful."

In 1994 he had a narrative dream of a very stressful situation. In it, he and a friend were walking out into the back yard of the home where he and our family had lived 30 years earlier.

Unexpected Precipice Behind Old House

I am at the house at Cameron Hill, NC, where Rachel and I and baby Marcia lived more than 30 years ago. Strangely, it has been coalesced into the first house that we lived in at Hampden-Sydney and thus is simultaneously in North Carolina and central Virginia. It is currently occupied by another faculty member, though not quite clear which one. I spend some time looking around inside the house. But then with the current occupant I go out into the backyard. We walk far out and down into the edge of woods where Rachel and I often walked while living at Cameron Hill. I find that many trees have been cleared away and suddenly we find ourselves at the edge of an enormous chasm, a nearly vertical drop off down a dirt embankment, many hundreds of feet above the valley floor. The ground is very soft and loose and I realize if I get too near the edge I will slip and fall and plummet down into the valley below. I do in fact begin to slip and find myself face down dangling over the edge, struggling to climb back up, but unable to do so. My friend tries to pull me up, but cannot do so alone. He leaves hurriedly to get help, leaving me with the assurance that when he comes back with enough people they can pull me up. I am content to hang on and wait. Then I wake up.

Not as obvious as some of the dreams recounted above, this dream takes some studying to decipher its message. People and places in dreams can have metaphorical as well as literal meanings. Only the dreamer himself, through his associations with the dream elements and the circumstances of his life, can establish a dream's true meaning. So what are these for him?

Owen recalled how his own father, in waking life, loved to go and sit by himself in their back yard. So, to him, " 'Back yard' is where you go when you want to get away from the world." He also stated it can represent "the deeper, lesser-known, more dangerous, perhaps unconscious aspects of my life, where you go deep down into yourself. The front yard is the more public part of life—facing the street—where you have to be open for business."

For him, the "chasm represents the danger of a loss of the self, the danger of personal and emotional annihilation, danger of 'losing it,' whether real or imaginary. The trustworthy friend going to get others, to get help to rescue me, perhaps symbolizes the reality of a genuinely caring and supportive community or the availability of friends and colleagues who also in fact care for me."

At the time of this dream, Owen was feeling stressed in a variety of ways. I had recently undergone surgery and treatments for breast cancer.

He had experienced difficult times connected to his job. He was troubled by many self-doubts. This dream was bringing him an important message of reassurance—that he has friends and colleagues who genuinely care for him, offer friendship, and are available to provide support in times of stress.

We can also remember that characters in a dream also represent aspects of oneself. So the friend in this dream also represents qualities within Owen that he can call upon to help himself.

It is easy to enjoy and appreciate dreams that portray beneficial experiences in tranquil and inviting settings. It is harder to feel grateful for ones like those discussed above. It is important to remember that all dreams come to us in the service of health and wholeness. We can be grateful, as was the dreamer of these dreams, when we are given seemingly stressful and disturbing dreams. They are bringing us guidance to help us on our journeys through life.

Reflections of Emotional Truths

Montague Ullman, M.D., with over 55 years of experience in working with dreams, stated at a dreamwork lecture that "dreams are magic mirrors that reflect back to us our emotional truth. Because of this capacity they serve our survival needs. Dreams start in the present with our current condition. Some event of the day triggers a dream because it is connected to some unfinished business of the past. Dreaming opens a remote memory bank and pulls out pieces that are emotionally connected to the present issue." He believed you can rely upon what it is saying about this issue. The following are some of my notes from his lecture:

When trying to help someone discover the meaning of a dream, there are several important questions one should ask the dreamer:

(1) Which people in the dream are "real" and which are unknown?

(2) What was the context in which the dream came to the dreamer? What was he thinking about, what was on his mind, right before going to sleep, during the few

hours before going to bed, and/or during the day? (If the dream is not a recent one, it may be hard to answer this. But recalling something about the time when the dream occurred may help.)

(3) What were his feelings about these things?

(4) What are his feelings about the images in the dream?

(5) What parts of the dreamer might be represented by the characters in the dream?

(6) How do his feelings about the characters in the dream correspond to his real life feelings about them in the past? If there is a difference between the two, what does this show? What is the dream saying to him about this?

Let's use Ullman's questions to explore one of Owen's dreams when he was in his late 60's.

Warmly Emotional Departure of Black Teenage Girl

My wife and I are standing with a lovely, late-teenage black girl, on something like a railway station platform. She has been staying with us for a while, though exactly how long and why are not clear; perhaps she is an exchange student, perhaps briefly in foster care. She does not appear to be troubled or in any difficulty. In any case, she is preparing to leave (return home? go back to school?); we have taken her to whatever will be her means of transportation, perhaps train or plane. As we are saying goodbye, I pull her to me for a hug rather than simply a handshake. She responds with evident warmth and pleasure, nestling very close to me, her head on my shoulder, for a prolonged embrace. I feel very

loving toward her, with much emotional warmth and
tenderness. Then I wake up.

I asked Owen the above questions. His answers to each question were as
follows:

(1) The man and his wife are "real." The black girl is an
unidentified, unknown person.

(2) He was not conscious of any particular thoughts right
before going to sleep, but during the evening he and I
had watched a biography of Oprah Winfrey on TV.

(3) While watching he felt deep compassion and
concern for Oprah and began to understand the difficult
circumstances that teenage black females have often
experienced.

(4) In the dream the main image (or character) other
than himself was the teenage black girl. He felt
"very loving toward her in a fatherly way, with much
emotional warmth and tenderness."

In a dream "real" people, especially close family members, may simply
represent themselves. Since unknown characters may represent a part of
oneself, I asked Owen what part the girl represented.

(5) The answer was "the 'anima,' the feminine part of
myself which I certainly would not have acknowledged
as a teenager. It might also be a 'shadow figure.'" In the
psychological language associated with Carl Jung, the
"anima" represents certain qualities of the inner male
self, often unconscious, that are typically associated
with the opposite sex but that are in fact important to
a mature and integrated masculine personality. The
"shadow figures" are characteristics, attitudes and

behaviors that may or may not actually be undesirable, which are repressed or suppressed in our formative years because they were considered unacceptable by our parents or other adults.

When asked, "What were your feelings as a teenager towards black females?" (6) he responded that he had been strongly influenced by traditional Southern stereotypes and prejudices.

This dream illustrates quite well two additional concepts given by Montague Ullman: "Dreaming consolidates recent learning. Dreams connect us to our past and to our behavior toward others now."

I then asked, "What do you feel the dream is saying to you?" (6) He responded that it points out an "understanding and acceptance of the feminine in myself that I once could not have acknowledged. On another level it shows a new awareness of the suffering many black teenagers have come through, as illustrated by the sense of genuine warmth toward someone toward whom as a teenager I would have harbored stereotypical and racist feelings rooted in my upbringing. There is nothing alien to my human nature about a person of another race. There is an essential oneness of the whole human family."

Retracing Steps to Resolve Issue

The more one works with dreams, the more one may realize the fact that dreams can help us understand our inner needs. Carl Jung described dreams as self-portraits, symbolic statements of what is going on in the personality from the point of view of the unconscious. Dreams may disclose unconscious motivations operating in relationships and may present new points of view in conflict situations. Bringing unconscious information to consciousness can help restore the psyche to a healthy balance, a process Jung called *individuation*. Once we understand what is going on, we can decide what we might do to help ourselves in this process.

Almost 20 years ago, as he was beginning to be aware of inner tensions, Owen had the following dream:

You Can Go Home Again, But No Shortcuts

We're leaving my boyhood house . . . the four of us,
the whole family, apparently at our current ages—all
adults. We drive down our road to the main road, and
turn right, as we always did. We go about a hundred
yards, and then I remember that we have left something
of importance at the house; it seems to have been a
blanket and possibly something of importance to my
daughter, but I'm not absolutely sure. We are in a
circa 1985 Plymouth Gran Fury—a dull, conventional
but extremely sturdy vehicle largely used by police
departments and taxi companies. My wife is driving.
We stop and I decide that I must go back to the house
to retrieve what has been left. But I will walk back on
my own to get it, while the family waits for me on the
highway in the car. I decide to try to take a short cut
instead of going back by the road. But find that this
will entail climbing up and over about a hundred-foot
mounted ridge of loose stone and earth. I climb to the
top of this and make my way to its farther edge and
find before me an extremely deep, vertical chasm that
I cannot possibly get across. So I climb back down
the stone heap and begin to jog back toward the road
leading back to the house. I have a feeling of energy
and contentment as I begin this return jog (about one-
quarter mile).

When asked what he thought the dream was showing, Owen replied:
"The car represents the strength and security of our family ties. [The car
in which the whole family is traveling is an 'extremely sturdy vehicle.']
The journey back to the house which I have to make by myself represents
the necessity of my retrieving and resolving issues from my childhood and
teen years . . . and then returning to the family before we can travel on
together. But I have to go back by the road that I have traversed so far. [He
must retrace his steps, go back over in his mind the path he has traveled in

his life.] I cannot take a short cut. There is not any quick sudden fix. [He cannot work through his issues quickly. He must go step by step by himself under his own power.] The sense that what I must retrieve has particular significance for my daughter may suggest that she has been the one most hurt by the unresolved tensions that I have carried with me."

There are three additional features of the dream that may be significant:

> 1. I am driving the car. This may be indicating that he felt he was not in control of what was happening at that point of his life; I was in the driver's seat. If this were my dream, I would see both negative and positive aspects in this. I might feel out of control, but my wife may have a better sense of direction. Also, I might represent his feminine-nurturing attributes. Therefore, this part of himself is capable of guiding his family in the right direction.

> 2. Owen remembered he needed to retrieve a blanket, an item of importance to our daughter. If this were my dream, I might relate the blanket to a security blanket our daughter had when she was little. I might ponder what issues from my own childhood might have affected her security and how.

> 3. As Owen was jogging back to the house he had "a feeling of energy and contentment." If this were my dream, I would notice that it feels right and energizing to be undertaking the "trip" back to resolve issues from childhood and teen years. Such an undertaking might lead to self-understanding and psychological inner balance. Dreams do not tell us what to do, but they offer suggestions. It is up to us to follow up In whatever way seems best to us.

A Source Providing More Insights

Still another of Owen's dreams that made reference to something from his childhood offered additional insight and provided encouragement. Owen had a "tunnel dream" in which he and I attended a gathering in a town similar to the one where he grew up. He recounted:

Isolated Road, Unexpected Tunnel, into Darkness

. . . The way we drove in seems somewhat crowded
and difficult, so we decide to leave by an open but
unfamiliar road in the opposite direction. Assuming
this is my hometown, I feel confident of being able to
find the way. But as we round a bend, the road, though
good, is in open country and begins winding up hilly
terrain toward mountains, with no sign of buildings or
other cars.

After driving a short distance farther, we round a curve
and immediately confront a tunnel with a rough stone
facing, much like a Blue Ridge Parkway tunnel. We are
concerned, but decide to go on through the tunnel. As
we begin to do so, we are suddenly on foot, no longer
in the car. The tunnel is very dark, with a bend some
distance ahead of us. The ceiling is low, so I have to
duck down a little. As we walk we do begin to see light
around the bend, at the end of the tunnel. We make our
way through it, and looking back at it from the far side
we see that it is neatly faced with brick, much less rustic
than the other end.

We emerge into what seems a settlement of some sort
along a road. But it is now late in the day, we have no
idea where we are, and I become very concerned about
our need to get back to where we came from before
dark. Darkness now is falling rapidly. I faintly see a few

walking figures, but they are too distant and obscure to
make contact with them. As it becomes completely dark,
I wake up.

If this were my dream, I might consider the tunnel a juncture between
the past—my hometown representing all that is familiar to me—and the
future—the unfamiliar settlement and figures beyond the tunnel. The
fact that I made it through the dark tunnel successfully under my own
power—on foot—would suggest that I had recently been exploring my
unconscious and probably had gained greater self-knowledge—the light
at the end of the tunnel. Although I was anxious to get back to what
was familiar before dark, it apparently wasn't possible and this can be
frightening. But I note that the tunnel on this side was "neatly faced with
brick, much less rustic than the other end." This might suggest a positive
outlook on the future.

—22—

A SPIRITUAL AUTOBIOGRAPHY

Dreams come from a deep "inner knowing" within ourselves and provide a connection to the Divine Source. Through dreams we can become aware of what matters to us. Concerns, which may have been below our conscious awareness, are revealed in our dreams. When we remember what we have dreamed, we are ready to look at this material, discover what really matters, and learn how we can respond (take some "action") in a beneficial manner.

Our homes—very common symbols in our dreams—often represent where we live mentally, emotionally, and spiritually. The addition of new rooms may suggest new ideas fitting within and expanding old belief systems. But when new ideas cannot fit within the old framework, we will see this represented in our dreams by the building of new houses or looking for a new house.

As I review my own dreams of many years, I see a picture of change and growth. In 1994 I dreamed of visiting an old house into which I planned to move. I found the basement filled with a lot of muck that was being cleaned out. The basement of a house often represents our unconscious mind. This dream seemed to be showing me that some of my basic beliefs—perhaps ones of which I was not fully conscious—were being cleared away. Then seven years later, in March of 2001, I dreamed I explored and discovered new additions and changes in our house and yard. This would indicate I was discovering or developing new abilities and/or ideas. In September of 2001 I dreamed of visiting my parents (who in waking life were no longer living) who had moved to a new city. Although I liked certain features of their house I discovered they occupied only the second floor. I decided this would not be a good place to live. The dream was saying I do not want to remain at the level of consciousness I developed as a child in my parents' household. I want to have access to what is metaphorically "below": I want to be grounded and to be able as an adult to explore the unconscious level. This can be facilitated through dreamwork.

The following January I dreamed

We Think Building Makes Sense Because We're Expecting a Baby

> Owen and I are planning to build a new home. The dream "situation/locale" doesn't resemble that of our waking life, but I do not recall any details. Some people think it is foolish for us to consider doing this since we already have such a nice house. But we think maybe it makes sense to do this because we're going to have a baby. (In waking life we were considering building, but we certainly weren't expecting a baby.)

A baby can be a symbol for something new coming into one's life. It can be any number of things, depending upon one's circumstances. Multiple levels of meaning can include actual events and new ideas and beliefs. Tracing the progression of just one of many symbols in my dreams—houses—shows a definite pattern of change and growth, as we saw in Chapter 7.

Understanding our dreams can also be approached in a different manner. Paula Reeves, a well-known therapist and lecturer in the fields of psychology and spirituality who led a session of the Group Dreamwork Training Institute that I attended in 2002, teaches our dreams are messages from our soul, "the incarnate essential Self." In her book *Women's Intuition: Unlocking the Wisdom of the Body*, she states: "Soul, that personal experience of the Ineffable, of the Self, has many forms of expression by which we can recognize its presence in our life. When it emanates from the psyche, it comes to us in dreams, in imagination, or in intuitive flashes."

At our session Reeves declared soul does not care about the individual facts of a dream; the essence of the dream gives its message. On Friday evening she asked us to go deep within ourselves to discern what our predominant feelings were at the moment. I wrote down "the paradox of anxiety and hope." We were then asked to keep this thought with us as we went to sleep and see if it influenced our dreams of the night.

The following morning I remembered three short dreams. The first dream expressed the emotion of anxiety; the second one expressed hope. The third dream was more intriguing. In it I observed a friend doing something that startled me and made me anxious for her. But at the end of the dream I felt more accepting and hoped everything would be all right. Reeves discussed each person's dream in turn. She asked me to state the essence of this third dream. After a few moments I said, "The unexpected can be acceptable."

The coming into consciousness of this phrase—"the unexpected can be acceptable," which resolves the paradox of anxiety and hope—illumined what seems to be a true pattern of my life. Looking back over many major events in my life I can see how they certainly were unexpected and often undesirable, but have been acceptable. Two or three years prior to having this dream I did not expect or want to be building another house in a particular locale. Not only did this become acceptable, it proved to be very desirable and enjoyable. I certainly did not expect my mother would die when I was only 32 years old and I would have a stepmother for more than 25 years. Although I wish this had not happened, I learned many valuable life lessons through this experience. I most certainly did not expect to get breast cancer, but the experience became a turning point in my life. This life threatening experience led me to reflect upon the meaning of my life, to consider what is important and what I am called to do. Not only can the unexpected be acceptable, even the unwanted, traumatic, anxiety-producing events can be true learning experiences—valuable steps in the process of individuation, the process of becoming the person one is meant to be.

Amazing Dream Revelations

During further review of dreams beginning in 1994, I discovered that some pointed out through the use of metaphor, sometimes quite urgently and dramatically, a need for some transition in my spiritual awareness and religious affiliation.

I grew up in the traditional, mainline Protestant denomination of my parents, joining this church as a teenager. Then when I married I joined my husband's denomination, thinking it would differ little from my familiar church. However, through the years I became uncomfortable with parts of its creedal emphasis. My maturing outlook felt the need of a different, more liberal and inclusive spiritual home.

A dream in 1994 suggested that my father and my husband have been the two strongest masculine and perhaps religious influences in my life. In the dream I declared I am not only my father's daughter, but also my husband's wife. Here is a slightly abbreviated account of the dream:

Being Shot At While Seeking Information

My husband and I are living in a new and unfamiliar community in a temporary dwelling. I decide to look for a particular shop. . . . We go to a nearby restaurant to ask someone how to find the shop. This is back of a large building that houses a church, dark and massive. Our planned future dwelling is an apartment on the backside of this large building. There are young girls— waitresses—at the restaurant. They are setting the tables in preparation for later use. I search for and find the woman in charge to ask her my question. She says, "Yes, there is a place and it is near the residence of So-and-So Owen Norment." I say we are the Owen Norments. This must be a relative. She replies, "No, you are Luther Gobbel's daughter." I say, "Yes, but I'm also Owen Norment's wife."

By this time we are outside between a restaurant and a church . . . with the restaurant's proprietress. . . . As I look back towards the large, dark church building I see a group of men in some kind of uniform gathering in an area next to the building. Suddenly, after suspicious activity by the men, something whizzes over our heads. We drop to the ground. More bullets (which can symbolize hard or hurtful words) whiz by. We try to

crawl on the ground to the safety of the columns of the
large building near us. We fear for our safety.

Then a new woman comes and evidently has business
with the restaurant's proprietress. I hear something
that sounds like the term "release." This woman has
been living where we are planning to move—a space
connected to the barny, massive church. The proprietress
is signing "release" papers for this woman. I think this
sounds as if the woman has been in prison and is being
let out, allowed to leave. (A part of me represented by
the woman is seeking and obtaining release from the
church.)

I question whether we should still think of living there.
I say, "It sounds as if the place is a prison, maybe we
should reconsider our plans." We may be unsuspectingly
planning to go to what is actually a prison.

This dream was bringing into my awareness an unacknowledged inner
fear about safety and feelings of constraint in connection with a church.
Perhaps "the men in uniform" were symbolic of patriarchal attitudes and
beliefs of the church and the uniforms were the common personas they—
and those related to the church— were required to wear. The bullets might
represent the creedal words that I felt were harmful. Thus I felt I would be
confined were I to become a part of that church.

Six months later, in a dream, we were

Attending a Religious Service

My husband and I go to a special religious service in
a large sanctuary. When seated in the very middle of
the front row, I fear being very conspicuous if I get
sleepy during the speech. The only part of the service
I remember is one in which some wine is served to my

husband. I am not offered any. I figure they know I
don't want any.

This last comment might be a rationalization. The fact that I was not offered
wine might point to the dream having meaning beyond the personal.
Historically women have often been banned from full participation in
certain religious ceremonies.

Almost three years later, in another dream,

The Breath is Being Squeezed Out of Me

I am sitting on a pew-like bench in a public building—
perhaps a church. There is a large fat man on my left and
a smaller person—perhaps a woman—on my right. This
latter person is on the end of the row. I feel I am being
"squeezed"—that I don't have room, that I can hardly
breathe. I plead, "Let me have room" or "Let me out so I
can have room to breathe"—or something to this effect.

What a dramatic plea to be allowed room to breathe! My inner Self felt
that the breath of life was being squeezed out of me. The next night I had
an even more dramatic and disturbing dream. Since it has already been
mentioned in Chapter 8, I'll just summarize how it begins:

I Ask the Man If I May Use the Commode

I am in a strange hotel room with a strange man, someone
I do not know. I need the bathroom. I ask the man if we
have a commode in our room. He reveals a commode
hidden behind a door. I ask if I may use the commode. He
is standing near it and will have to move out of the way if
I'm to use it. He says it's okay and moves. . . .

This is the dream that was discussed with Jeremy Taylor. He felt a deep part
of me was expressing the need to give free expressions to my feelings in the
world and my need to experience spirituality in whatever way I desire. The

rest of the dream showed the consequences of not having free expression. It contained a series of very explicit scenes in which I was a captive being led around by males and, along with other females, being sexually exploited. Taylor believes that when sex appears unmasked in a dream it is a symbol of something else. It is showing symbolically one's interior spiritual state, in this case one in which the dreamer feels exploited. The dream is about unfulfilled spiritual longings for conscious connection to the Divine shown in metaphors of sexual content.

Learning the message of this dream was beneficial on several levels. I had been very disturbed by this and other dreams depicting explicit sexual exploitation. Having been to several workshops and a conference led by Taylor I had confidence in his ability to help people understand their dreams. Since he was the guest facilitator at this session of the Group Dreamwork Training Institute at which it was my turn to have a dream discussed, I decided this would be my dream. But I still worried about sharing it and I slept very little the night beforehand. I felt a tremendous relief after hearing the discussion. It also proved to be beneficial to the other participants. Many of them thanked me afterwards for sharing it.

A year and a half after this dream I joined a church where I felt more spiritually and theologically at home. However, a year after that my psyche was still wrestling with the question of my church membership, as seen in the following dream:

I'm Being Pressured to Go to a Church Service I Don't Want to Attend

In the dream, as I wake up fairly late one morning a member of my family quickly asks me to be ready to go to a church service that morning with them. "How soon does it begin?" I ask. Probably within 20-30 minutes or less. I have not dressed, nor have I had anything to eat. I really wanted to go to a different service later. My father is probably the one urging me to go. I try to make excuses. It becomes apparent that the service is to be held in a large room near our rooms. I'm led to the doorway to look in. I see that some members of my family are already seated. I really don't want to go, but I

feel under great pressure to join them. I finally agree to
go. I wake up before I do go.

My inner psyche felt pressured by my "family." In this dream it seemed to
be my family of origin; my father was the one urging me to go to a church
service I did not want to attend. Evidently I continued working through
the question in my unconscious for another year and a half. Then my
dreammaker acknowledged my shift with this dream:

We Take Our Daughter to Visit My New Church

Our daughter is visiting and we decide to take her to
visit my new church. When we go, we are attending a
church meeting—seemingly not a Sunday service—at
which the minister is introducing the various leaders,
maybe committee chairs. . . . I have assumed that we
will simply be told what each person's duty is. I'm
surprised when we are instructed to put seats in a circle
and sit to observe an actual meeting of the leaders, who
take their seats in the circle also. Thus I feel accepted as
a full participant, part of the circle, with the prospect of
ongoing learning and involvement.

This dream occurred 11 years ago. Not recalling additional dreams on
this subject during the years since this one, I decided I would search
through subsequent dreams to see if my psyche was satisfied with this
outcome. I discovered at least a dozen more dealing with this subject. I
had not thought I'd find many; however, I am not surprised to know that
my spiritual journey has been ongoing. These dreams reveal a continuing
search for a church I want to attend. I will summarize a dream that came
three months after the last dream above, in November 2001.

I Don't Want to Attend the Church

I am headed to attend a particular church (different
from the one I joined in waking life), but I feel reluctant

to go. I make an excuse for not wanting to go. Even after discovering the excuse is invalid, I still don't want to go—and don't.

The most striking of these newly discovered dreams occurred two and a half months later.

I Refuse to Participate in Some Secret Church Ceremony and Am Glad I Refused

I go with Owen to a church meeting in an unidentified place. He has been asked there in an official role, but I don't know, in the dream, just what he is expected to do. He goes inside the meeting room. I wait outside in a hall. After a while I go to the door, thinking I'll just glance inside. Some man comes out and tells me he wants me to come in to be part of whatever is taking place. I inquire just what will be involved. He won't tell me. He takes my arm and tries to usher me in. I resist, asking again what it is I'll have to do. He won't say. I get the impression that there is some secret ceremony that involves something being done to the participant. I tell him I won't do it. He'll have to find someone else. With that I pull away from him and go away from the door.

Sometime later the man comes out where I am. Now there are other people around. He makes a loud comment for all to hear: "Some women won't do what you ask them to do." I know the comment is aimed at me. I immediately retort loudly, "Some churches expect people to do what they ask without questioning it." He leaves and goes back into the meeting.

Later I'm with Owen and we are in or go into a room where a man is brought in on a gurney. He appears to be only half conscious, seemingly coming out from under some drug. He was the person who took part in the "ceremony." I'm thankful I refused to participate. I certainly don't want to be given a drug or medication—one they won't even identify in advance. I had heard that perhaps the participants were given some antibiotics. I don't want to take any of them needlessly either.

Wow! I think this dream clearly stated what my psyche thought of certain patriarchal and clerical ideas and attitudes. In addition to not wanting to be drugged, I was/am unwilling to participate in activities—church-related or otherwise—that are not fully explained—revealed—to me in advance. My mind is open, but questioning; I want to know and understand concepts and procedures.

Two months later, in April 2002, I'm still questioning

Church-Related Activities

I am attending a church-related meeting or possibly a church service. I am helping in some capacity, perhaps singing in the choir. Most of the details have left my memory. I believe I am questioning in my mind whether to continue participating here. On one occasion my father has been here with me. He seems not to think very highly of what has been taking place. He may advise me to go elsewhere (not sure). Then he walks away from the place. . . .

Although I did not recall whether his attitudes and beliefs caused me to decide against continuing participation at this church (in the dream), apparently I was still experiencing some input from my father. Attitudes and beliefs heard and perhaps "absorbed" during childhood can linger, at least unconsciously, long after one begins to consciously question them. This dream was bringing this awareness back into my consciousness.

The next dream in the series, *My Family Is Expecting Me to Join Them at Church*, occurring eight months later, in December 2002, showed I was still feeling the pull/pressure from family. Then in a January 2003 dream I was still searching for a church home; I was visiting two different churches, located side by side, trying to decide between them. I did not like what I saw at the first one. Then I was pleased when I was warmly welcomed by a male friend at the second one.

In the next dream of the series, in February 2003, I was under another form of pressure.

I Am Being Detained by a Man Who Intends to Handcuff Me

> I'm in the passenger seat of a car driven by an unidentified man. Another woman is in the back seat. We are about to go into a building—maybe a country church—where the man is to be in charge of some event—perhaps a "social." The man intends to handcuff me before we go in. I believe he fears I will try to leave if he doesn't do something to stop me. I don't remember any details leading up to this that would explain the situation. I, of course, don't want to be handcuffed and try a stalling tactic to try to avoid it. I begin fumbling around in my pocketbook, saying I'm looking for something I need (forget what) before I get out. The man (surprisingly) allows me to do this. I thought he might refuse and demand I get out immediately, with him handcuffing me as I get out. He does get anxious to be getting on into the building to get things ready. So much so that he allows me to get out without his handcuffing me. We go into the building and he begins setting out supplies for the occasion. I'm trying to figure out a way I can get away or at least keep from being handcuffed. I try to look like I'm being helpful, suggesting a way to do something while gathering whatever is needed. It may be at this point that Owen appears and I assume he won't let the man handcuff me.

Again I was feeling pressured by a male to do something/go to a church social. This male might represent the pressures I have felt from males in my life. They could also represent masculine, or patriarchal, energies within myself. Did I not want to participate in that particular church's activities? It would be helpful if I could recall any waking-life circumstances at the time of the dream. For this reason it is helpful to record any pertinent "Day Notes" along with the dreams in your journals. I have not been as diligent about this in recent years as I was for many years.

The next four dreams in this series described a variety of situations that I found unpleasant and/or undesirable in connection with several churches. Obviously I was still contemplating the question of church affiliation during these years. In September 2004, in waking life I was still a participating member in the church I joined in 1999. However, the following dream expressed dissatisfaction.

I'm Irritated that My Church Has Their Records Confused

I have received some notice from my church. They
are asking me to join the church. As well as I can tell,
they seem to assume that by joining I will commit
to giving them larger monthly contributions. I'm
discussing this with someone, maybe Owen. I'm
upset—irritated—about the matter. In the first place
I'm already a member, thus they don't seem to have their
records straight. Secondly, I'm not going to increase the
amount I'm giving; I've already explained this to them.
Evidently they have forgotten that we are splitting our
contributions between two different churches.

Five years later a dream metaphorically depicted my continuing search for new insights.

Hunting for a Replacement for a Broken Lens of My Glasses

Owen and I have been attending a group meeting at a
small unfamiliar (to us) church. On one occasion we
are waiting for activity to begin and I wander around,
perhaps into the other side of the room, and perhaps

speak to someone. Somehow (?) my glasses come off
and one lens get crushed. I reach down and pick up
the pieces, carry them back to where we were sitting,
and show them to Owen. At first I think I'll wait until
later to get it replaced. But while we're waiting for the
meeting to start someone (?) urges me to go on to see
about getting the lens replaced.

At some point I'm aware that the minister of this small
church is sitting in the far back corner of the room. He
seems to be sitting there quietly, just observing what is
going on while waiting, as we are, for other activity to
take place. We nod a greeting to each other.

I go out the nearby door and wander into a different
part of the building. I seem to think I'll find a
repairman somewhere in this building. I go down a
short side hall, but don't find anyone who can help.

As I am leaving the meeting place with a female friend,
and we are not far away, I look back and see a large bus
pull into the driveway by the church. I realize it has
come to take us somewhere. . . . I think I need to hurry
to get back.

As my friend and I are traveling down a highway, I
become aware that two men are following us, maybe
on a motorcycle. I wonder if they are aware of us and
are deliberately following us. I become very uneasy
and begin to fear for our safety. I'm relieved when they
finally pass us.

As I pointed out in Chapter 5, glasses can symbolize the lens though
which we look at life—our outlook on life. In this dream one of my
lenses gets broken while in an unfamiliar church. Some aspect of my
outlook is destroyed. What caused this is not revealed. After I am urged

by someone, perhaps my husband, to seek replacement without waiting, I am unsuccessful in finding help at that church. The minister and I only greet each other with a nod. He does nothing that is helpful; apparently he does not even offer to help. This part of the dream can be considered on several levels: The minister of a church could not provide me with help in my spiritual undertakings or provide new insights. He might represent masculine energies that I considered "pushy," overbearing and threatening in a way similar to some seen in earlier dreams. Or, the minister might represent the masculine aspects within myself with which I am not comfortable. Do I still worry that someone might consider me too aggressive and out-of-line—going beyond what is considered "proper" for a female in our society?

While continuing my search outside the church, I become alarmed when two men follow us for a while. Perhaps something about my masculine energies caused me to feel threatened. This dream invites me to look within to discover what these concerns are, so I may understand them, accept them, and then incorporate the beneficial form of the energies into my life.

I am also invited to question what part of my outlook was destroyed. Was it something that needs to be changed? If so, how will this affect my spiritual search? What can replace the lens to help me have clearer vision as I continue my ongoing journey?

As I went to bed after writing the above passage, I did not have the answer to any of the questions. The next morning I awoke recalling a fragment of a dream:

The Group Leader's Son Is Sent Ahead to Make Arrangements

I am with a group of people. We are undertaking a journey on foot. The dream gives an extensive account of various activities, circumstances, and stops we make along the way. However, upon awaking I am unable to recall many details, including our destination and reason for making the journey. The one detail I do remember is that at one point the female leader of the group decides to send her adult son ahead to make arrangements for us all. He has to go to a different location, not our final destination, to make these arrangements. He will eventually meet us at our destination.

As I consider this dream I realize it gives me a suggestion regarding the questions I wrote yesterday about "Broken Lens" dream above. That dream suggested I could use my masculine energies to help me on my journey. This last dream suggests that I can use my masculine—positive assertive, outgoing, "doing"—energies to promote and accomplish my goals; I need not be reluctant to use them for beneficial purposes. This dream is an excellent example of a follow-up dream that helps one understand a prior dream. As someone else stated: It's a "great example of the value of ongoing dreamwork and the psyche's desire to answer a reflective ego's questions."

My inability to remember many details of this dream is not a problem. As Paula Reeves says, the essence of the dream gives its message and this is what I was able to remember.

The Roles We Play

In *As You Like It* William Shakespeare says, "All the world's a stage, And all the men and women merely players; And one man in his time plays many parts. . . ." Many of our dreams seem to echo this theme. In this context we can think of our lives as being productions of some kind. Our dreams of rehearsing for a play, movie, or musical production suggest preparations for new roles. As is true of all dreams, to discover the dream's message one needs to draw a parallel between the dream and waking reality by asking, "What is like that in my waking life?"

Since all characters in a dream represent some aspect of myself, when I am watching a production in a dream, the thoughts, feelings, hope and fears expressed by each character in the play are my own. I may not consciously know I think or feel these ways. Other dreams describe rehearsals for productions—musicals, dramas, dance, and films. In them, various aspects of myself of which I may not be conscious are rehearsing their roles in the production of my life. The dreams come to me from my dreammaker, a deep inner knowing that connects me with the Divine

Source, when it is time for me to become conscious of the roles these aspects are playing in my life.

Since I was engaged in a search for my life's purpose, it makes sense that one theme that appeared in my dreams at this time was that of seeking roles in some kind of productions. In connection with this theme, another typical dream is one in which the dreamer forgets his/her lines in a play. I had many dreams about forgetting my lines. The quote below is just a small part of a very lengthy and complicated dream:

I Don't Remember My Lines

> . . . The opening night I am panicked. I literally cannot
> remember what my opening line is. I am frantically
> trying to get someone to give me a copy of the script so
> my memory can be jarred. . . .

This dream suggests that somewhere in my inner being I knew the role—perhaps I knew what I am meant to do in this life, but it had not yet come into consciousness. Two weeks later I dreamed

I'm Told I'm Perfect the Way I Am for a Role in the Film

> Someone comes up to me and asks if I would like to
> be in a movie they are going to start filming. They are
> going to keep looking for other people for the cast, but
> they think I am probably the right person for one part.
> While they continue looking, I am to follow around
> with them. They inform me that it isn't a "big name"
> movie, just a locally made one. At one point I am told
> that I shouldn't change anything about myself, that I
> am just perfect the way I am. . . .

In this dream I was already wearing the kind of dress needed for the role. Often, in dreams, clothing represents one's *persona*, Jung's term for how we present ourselves to others. It was during this time that I was seeking my role in life and I began to have dreams regarding a commitment to service. This dream was trying to reassure me that what I had been doing was preparing me for a new role; I didn't need to do anything differently. But, of course, I did not realize it at the time.

In some dreams I auditioned for a certain part. In others, a role was offered unexpectedly. I turned down such a role in a dream in 1995:

I'm Expected to Play the Female Lead Role
Which I Can't Figure Out and Don't Want

I walk into a gathering of people, which appears to be a choral rehearsal. I'm the only woman there when I arrive. There are several men. They want the rehearsal to begin. It appears this is the initial rehearsal for a musical play. I discover that they expect me to sing the female lead role. I can't figure out where that part is on the "script." They start the rehearsal and expect me to sing the lead part where it appears, but I can't figure it out. I realize I really don't want to do the role. I finally announce that I just can't do it; they'll have to find someone else. I believe another woman has arrived at the rehearsal. Finally the very young woman agrees to take the part. She is much more suited for the role.

There are times when we feel pressured to undertake activities we don't think are right for us and we really don't want to do them. This dream was encouraging me to express my true feelings and desires.

Seven years later I turned down a role in another dream:

I Decide Not to Accept the Lead Female Role in the Musical

. . . At first I'm very pleased. But as time for rehearsals approaches, I begin to reconsider. . . . I decide it's more than I want to do. I seek out the producer and ask who will be the director; I feel I should go to him and tell him I'm withdrawing from the production. . . .

When asked why I would be turning down a good role being offered, in the dream I responded, "I want to choose which role I play. I don't want to be told what part I have to play in life."

Shakespeare said we each play many different roles. Sometimes we do this unconsciously. Our troubled inner child will act out. Our needy inner baby will plead for attention or we may feel and act like an abandoned orphan. At times we might act like the winner of a grand prize or, on the other end of the scale, like the loser in a reality show. However, we may also deliberately assume a particular role, perhaps to make a favorable impression upon someone hoping to benefit in some way. Or, just for the fun of it, we may try out very different roles. In 1994 I dreamed of volunteering for the role of "Salome."

Volunteering for the Role of "Salome"

... They need someone to do a "Salome" type dance in the pageant. No one has volunteered to even try out for the role. I decide it will be fun, so I volunteer. It will be another "different" role for me. I remember what fun it was to be "Bloody Mary" in "South Pacific." People didn't expect me to have that kind of part. ...

The dream went on to state I tried out even though I didn't expect to be given the part. This showed willingness to explore/try out new roles in my life, perhaps something different from what might be expected by others. It also made reference to something that had actually taken place in waking life. In 1985 I had great fun playing "Bloody Mary" in a community theater production of "South Pacific." I remember someone asking me afterwards what I thought of playing such a role. The unspoken implication was that since I am a minister's wife I might consider it objectionable to have the role of a person who would call someone else a bastard. Even though I might not use rough language in waking life, it was fun to portray such a different character in a musical.

When we moved away from the college community we had lived in for 30 years, I felt one of the benefits for me would be the new opportunities in a new environment. I would be able to undertake new avenues, perhaps in areas quite different from those people associated with me and/or expected of me.

In 1998, two years after the move, I had a dream in which both my husband and I were given roles in a production. In it

*I Don't Have a Script for the Play and Seek
One; Owen Has Been Given One*

> . . . My husband is to have a larger role than mine.
> I'm very unsure of just when I'm to do my part. I
> have not been given a copy of the script. In the dream
> I'm surprised to learn it's about time to give the
> production. . . . I try to look at my husband's copy
> of the script, but this really isn't sufficient. I think I
> should go back to get one for myself. . . . I make an
> unsuccessful trip back to get a script, and then return.
> I'll just have to muddle through, hoping I'll figure out
> or be told when I'm supposed to do something.

In thinking about this dream, Owen and I decided that since he was nearing retirement in waking life, his having the script pointed out that he has known his role in life for years and it has been a "major" role for him. Then, even though I had a successful career also, I felt there was a further role I am supposed to play and I was still in the process of learning what this was to be.

Just recently when I reread the chapter in Jean Raffa's *The Bridge to Wholeness* on "The Feminine Quest," I experienced a big "aha." This dream seems to illustrate what she describes as the basic difference between the masculine and feminine journeys to wholeness. She states that men need to develop and test their personal skills in the outer realm [world] before they are able to generate a connection with the inner world. But the opposite is true for women. Inner work is our primary task before we can "acquire a meaningful connection with the outer world." She continues, "Perhaps this explains why so many men seem to make their most noticeable contributions to the outer world in their early years and then retire to lives of quiet contemplation in later years." She gives several examples of men who she feels proved themselves in the outer world during the youthful years. Then she explains, "Perhaps their later, less visibly active years were spent in inner work, then completing the cycle to wholeness."

She goes on to explain that the feminine quest takes a different route. "For most women, the journey does not begin in the outer world. A woman may be extremely effective at her work—certainly she can compete and produce as well as men—but as long as she continues to follow the masculine model of the hero myth without doing her inner work, she is doomed to frustration. . . . A woman can find status in the outer world, but if she is seeking wholeness, she must go inward. . . . Once she gets in touch with her unconscious world and learns how to be true to her Self, she discovers how to express her unique talents and skills in meaningful ways in the outer world, while at the same time maintaining meaningful relationships."

My dreams and my life experiences make so much sense now. As I have stated, I did have a successful career in teaching, painting, and exhibiting. But I felt there was something more I was meant to do. Several years before this dream, Owen and I had begun inner work through dream work, counseling, and individual study. While Owen was approaching the concluding years of his major life work, I felt more creative avenues were opening up for me.

Searching for Life's Purpose

In early 1991 I began a conscious search for what more I should be doing with my life, beyond my career as a professional artist and teacher and my family life. I felt there was something else of great importance I am meant to be doing and I was impatient to know what it was. Although I expressed the desire to help others in some way, there remained many questions as to how this might be accomplished. I discovered the following significant series of dreams during my review of dreams. In a dream in February 1992,

I Want to Be Told What I'm Supposed to Teach

I am told I have to go back to teaching. This time I am to be teaching in an elementary school. I'm not at

all happy about this. When the first day arrives, I still
don't know exactly what I am to teach. I meet with
the administrators and ask just what am I to teach.
Instead of telling me I am to teach "art"—or to teach
the ordinary grade work, they simply pick up a brush
or some other painting tool and proceed to show me a
particular process I am to teach. I know the process; I
feel this is elemental. The process can be used to reach a
variety of goals. I assume the school wants the students
to reach certain goals so they can progress from one
level to the next, but I have not been told what the goals
are. I want to be told.

I was told I was to teach in an elementary school—a place of basic learning.
Although I had taught in the elementary grades thirty years before this
dream, I didn't think I was being told to go back into a second or third
grade classroom. Also, I didn't think I had been given enough information.
I wanted to know the goals I would be guiding students toward. I was
frustrated not to know specifics immediately.

I think this dream was saying I knew my new role in life would
involve teaching some basic information, but I didn't yet know how what
I would teach would help my students. I didn't have sufficient information
about the goals of the instruction. In waking life, I had just begun my
serious study of dreams when I had this dream. At this point I had no
idea how dreamwork could/can be a valuable guiding light during our life
journeys.

Two months later I dreamed I have gone to a public meeting where

I Meet a Very Special Woman

I have gone to a public meeting or gathering with one
or two family members. . . . The guest of honor—or
guest speaker—is a very special woman, someone such
as Mother Teresa. . . . We are standing or sitting in rows
waiting for her arrival. I am on the second or third row
from the front. As she arrives, she walks directly towards

us. In fact, she comes directly to me, extends her hand
to shake my hand, and commends me for having come
out to see her. I am very honored. I am the only one to
whom she extends this honor. I am dressed with a scarf
over my head.

This woman was honoring me by shaking my hand for some reason that
was not spelled out in the dream. Perhaps she was aware that I had made
a commitment to "service," to helping others. Or perhaps by coming to see
her I was signifying such a commitment. The gathering could even have
been for the purpose of taking part in a ritual of commitment.

I take this gathering to be spiritually significant for two reasons. One
reason was the presence of the "Mother Teresa" figure. The other is the fact
that I was wearing a scarf over my head. In certain religious traditions for a
woman to cover or veil her head is a sign or token of spiritual submission,
humility, and reverence. We need to remember that our dreams are coming
from a "deep inner knowing" within ourselves—a part that is connected
to the Divine Source. This was not a literal recounting of a waking-life
experience. However, it was a very significant event taking place in my
unconscious.

But I still I didn't know what I was to teach. Three weeks later I had
a dream that gave a little more information.

I Am to Give a Demo to Women that May Save Lives

I am with a group of people. Each person has selected
something they are supposed to "do." What I choose
is somewhat strange. I am to give a demo (not an art
demo) or instruction of some kind to women. I believe
it is important for me to do whatever it is because it
possibly will save lives.

We know that sometimes dream scenarios are exaggerations to get the
dreamer's attention, to bring a very important idea into his/her conscious
awareness. This dream seemed to be speaking to the question that this
series was addressing—what I'm supposed to be "doing." Even though

whatever I chose might not actually save someone's life, the point was it was something very important. The ego in this dream thought the choice was "strange." This dream occurred almost two years before my diagnosis of breast cancer. I was just beginning a serious study of dreamwork and certainly, at this stage, I had no notion I would some day teach people how to explore their dreams.

Then one dream immediately following my cancer diagnosis in 1994, part of the "initial dream series," suggested I would have something to contribute at a conference.

The Group Leader Thinks I Can Contribute to a Future Session

> There is a group of people who have participated in the
> conference and who have been with a particular man
> in a small discussion group. The man is arranging seats
> and is either putting name signs on the seats or making
> a list of people to take part in a future session with him.
> He sees me and decides to include me in his group. He
> is choosing people he thinks will be interested and good
> contributors to the discussions and sessions. He wants
> me to be a part of it.

It pleased me, in the dream and when I thought about it later, to think the man felt I might have something to contribute. However, at the time of the dream (while I was being treated for breast cancer) I had no idea what this could mean.

Looking back, I see that this dream came true at the Journey into Wholeness Dream Conference I attended soon after completing radiation therapy. At that conference I shared two of my significant dreams during a dream group session led by Jeremy Taylor, a co-founder of the International Association for the Study of Dreams and one of the three leaders and principal speakers of the conference. I sought clarification and understanding regarding several disturbing dreams I had during my cancer experience. The dream group session was an incredible experience during which I both learned a lot and was able to contribute to the group's learning experience. The dreams seemed very meaningful to others in the group;

many thanked me for telling my dreams and recounting my experiences relating the dreams and cancer. A medical doctor and a counselor asked for permission to use my experience anonymously in teaching their students.

I understand now that this last dream had an additional meaning: I can continue to contribute in my life beyond the cancer experience in several ways. But at the time I did not know how I might be able to do this. The idea that I could be of service was emphasized in another dream in September 1995.

I Have On the Wrong Color Robe

> At some point I'm to attend a meeting, perhaps a church service. I have on a black choir robe. As I go to a doorway to go in, I sense something is wrong. I'm not sure whether I have come to the wrong door. Then I learn that I have on the robe for . . . a different service (from the one just about to take place)—that the robe for this service is a purple one. I see some people with purple robes on inside the church sanctuary.

Deep inner wisdom, what I have been calling "my dreammaker," was telling me to take off the black robe of the unknown, the mysterious, and even the fear of death. I needed to put on the purple robe of healing abilities and spiritual strength and vitalities, and then go join others in the sanctuary for the service, a dream metaphor for the service I might offer to others.

These dreams were recorded in my journal and forgotten until I reviewed my dreams while writing my first book. I was surprised to discover that my dreams from years before the cancer diagnosis suggested that I have been following a path, unconsciously, preparing me for the main purpose of my life, my vocation, one of service. As I recount in *Guided by Dreams*, the unexpected trauma of breast cancer became the gateway to this.

Seven years later, in 2002, I was studying, learning all I could about dreams, hoping that what I was doing was somehow preparing me for my special role. I was impatient to know what it was. I dreamed

I Want to Learn What My Role Will Be in the Next Play

> I'm attending a gathering of community players—
> perhaps at a two- or three-day occasion—where I believe
> plans for an upcoming production will be discussed.
> I even expect we will be given our assignments as to
> what our roles will be. Nothing of this sort seems to be
> taking place. I keep waiting to learn what my role is to
> be. . . . Later I ask the person in charge why we haven't
> been given our parts for the next play. I forget the exact
> response, but the gist is that it's not time for that. This
> meeting is for more general preparations, inspiration, etc.

I take note of the reason given for our not being given information about our next roles: it was not time for that yet. In the meantime we were being given inspiration and basic preparations. I had been told by a counselor long ago, in waking life, that I would know when the time was right.

I know now that I began to undertake the new role—my vocation—when I began teaching people how to understand their dreams soon after the Journey into Wholeness Dream Conference. Ever since then I have been facilitating workshops and small dream groups where participants may explore their own dreams.

In addition to dreaming of being an actor in a play, we may sometimes dream of being the director. Here's an example:

I Make Up the Action as I Direct the Production; I Ask the Group to Help

> I'm in a large group setting where I am the instructor,
> director of some production that we are to give soon.
> I'm making up the action as we go along. At the same
> time persons involved are following these directions. We
> have done this one day and are coming back a second
> day to continue rehearsing. I had not written down the
> instructions, so I'm trying to remember them again.
> At some point I ask the group to help me out, saying,

"Come on, help me out here"—help me recall the
actions we decided on the day before. I ask someone to
start writing down the action. . . .

I called (my ego called) upon all parts of myself (the group who worked
with me to create the presentation) to help me remember the preplanned
script—what we had already discussed (what was already in my awareness).
What was left unsaid was the need to bring up additional important
information still buried deep within my unconscious. The dream *I Accept
the Role of Doctor* (described in Chapter 19) came in 1999, a year after this
dream. Even after having that dream I still wasn't sure of my role, as this
dream and several others revealed.

My quest evidently was following the path of the feminine quest
described by Jean Raffa (as discussed a few pages above). I was, and am,
seeking wholeness by going inward to get in touch with my unconscious
world. Through contemplation of what I am learning by this means and
during extensive study and daily experiences I am discovering how best to
express my "talent and skills in meaningful ways in the outer world."

This last dream has a message for us all. We are the creator of our lives;
we can write the script and direct our lives. With mindful application of
this ability, guided by our dreams coming from a "deep inner knowing,"
we can make great strides along our journeys of individuation.

Dreamwork has become my passion. I am convinced of the importance
of listening to and honoring the Divine messages our dreams bring us.
We honor a dream when we undertake any form of working with the
dream, such as recording it, drawing it, meditating on insights gained, and
following suggestions offered through its symbols and metaphors, with
appreciation and the intention to bring the dream's healing energies into
waking life. Dreams can help us understand ourselves, help us to grow in
mind, body and spirit. True fulfillment comes when we can feel we are
doing something for which we are best qualified and prepared, something
we feel we are being called to do with our lives. It takes some of us longer
than others to know what our special calling is. Our revelatory dreams
are sometimes startling, often amazing. If we will pay attention to them,
they will help us on our journeys toward healing and wholeness and the
realization of our potential.

AFTERWORD

For a long time I considered calling this book *The Cat's Meow: Finding One's Voice with the Aid of Dreams.* A cat or kitten has been a symbol for myself for many years. At one point, as I discussed in Chapter 14, I began to have dreams in which a cat actually spoke—at first just one word, then gradually a phrase or two, and finally in full sentences. I feel this was showing that I have been gradually finding my voice, finding a way to express myself and to fulfill my potential during this lifetime.

This experience in dream exploration has heightened my appreciation of how valuable the information gained through dreamwork can be.

The process of learning about ourselves (*self-knowledge*) and developing our potential to become balanced, healthy and "whole" (*self-realization*) is ongoing throughout our entire lives. It doesn't happen all at once. First we become aware of and acquainted with unknown parts of ourselves. When we acknowledge and accept all parts, we can transform previously unknown energies into creative energies that can help bring our psyches into balance.

Very likely you will not examine in detail each and every dream at the time you record them. So, it is very important to undertake periodic reviews, searching for recurring themes and images. You can explore the similar and recurring themes, as I have in this book, discovering amazing things about yourself, gaining much self-knowledge that can lead to self-realization. This is the process Jung called *Individuation.* Dreams provide us with a helpful means of discovering the unknown and learning where we are on our journey towards wholeness. May we be open to the challenge. It is a great adventure.

APPENDIX:
DREAM CONTENTS BY TITLES

BIBLIOGRAPHY

Andrews, Ted. *Animal-Speak: The Spiritual & Magical Powers of Creatures Great & Small.* St. Paul, MN: Llewellyn Publications, 1997.

_____. *Animal-Wise: The Spirit Language & Signs of Nature.* Jackson, TN: Dragonhawk Publishing, 1999.

_____. *Nature-Speak: Signs, Omens, & Messages in Nature.* Jackson, TN: Dragonhawk Publishing, 2004.

Barasch, Marc Ian. *Healing Dreams: Exploring the Dreams That Can Transform Your Life.* New York: Riverhead Books, 2000.

Bolen, Jean Shinoda. *Crossing to Avalon.* New York: HarperCollins, 1994.

Boone, J. Allen. *Kinship With All Life.* New York: HarperSanFrancisco, 1954.

Burch, Wanda. *She Who Dreams: A Journey into Healing Through Dreamwork.* Novato, CA: New World Library, 2003.

Bush, Carol. *Healing Imagery & Music.* New York: Sterling, 1999.

Callanan, Maggie and Patricia Kelley. *Final Gifts.* New York: Simon & Schuster, 1992.

Campbell. Jean. *Group Dreaming: Dreams to the Tenth Power.* Norfolk, VA: Wordminder Press, 2006.

Cheung, Theresa. *The Element Encyclopedia of 20,000 Dreams.* New York: Harper Element, 2006.

_____. *The Dream Dictionary from A to Z.* New York: Harper Element, 2008.

Clift, Jean Dalby and Wallace B. Cliff. *The Hero Journey in Dreams.* New York: Crossroad Publishing, 1991.

Crisp, Tony. *Your Dream Interpreter.* Pleasantville, NY: Reader's Digest, 2005.

Davis, Elizabeth and Carol Leonard. *The Circle of Life.* Berkeley, CA: Celestial Arts, 2002.

Garfield, Patricia. *The Healing Power of Dreams.* New York: Simon & Schuster, 1991.

————. *The Universal Dream Key: The 12 Most Common Dream Themes Around the World.* New York: HarperCollins, 2001.

Getty, Adele. *Goddess: Mother of Living Nature.* New York: Thames & Hudson, 2001.

Gordon, David. *Mindful Dreaming: A Practical Guide for Emotional Healing Through Transformative Mythic Journeys.* Franklin Lakes, NJ: Career Press, 2007.

Gore, Al. *An Inconvenient Truth.* New York: Rodale, 2006.

Goldhammer, John D. *Radical Dreaming: Use Your Dreams to Change Your Life.* New York: Kensington Publishing, 2003.

Gratton, Nicole and Monique Sequin. *Dreams and Death: The Benefits of Dreams Before, During and After Death.* Canada: 2011.

Guiley, Rosemary Ellen. *Dreamwork for the Soul.* New York: Penguin Putman, 1998.

————. *Dreamspeak.* New York: Penguin Putman, 2001.

Holloway, Gillian. *The Complete Dream Book: Discover What Your Dreams Tell You about You and Your Life.* Naperville, IL: Sourcebooks, 2001.

Hoss, Robert J. *Dream Language.* Ashland, OR: Innersource, 2005.

Johnson, Robert. *Inner Work: Using Dreams and Active Imagination for Personal Growth.* San Francisco: Harper & Row, 1983.

Judith, Anodea and Selena Vega. *The Sevenfold Journey.* Berkeley, CA: Ten Speed Press, 1993.

Jung, Carl G. *Memories, Dreams, Reflections.* New York: Random House, 1963.

Kabat-Zinn, *Full Catastrophe Living: Using the Wisdom of Our Body and Mind to Face Stress, Pain, and Illness.* New York: Bantam Dell, 1990.

Keck, L, Robert *Healing As a Sacred Path: A Story of Personal, Medical, and Spiritual Transformation.* West Chester, PA: Chrysalis Books, 2002.

Larsen, Stephen. *The Mythic Imagination: The Quest for Meaning Through Personal Mythology.* New York: Bantam Dell, 1996.

Lohff, David C. *The Dream Dictionary.* Philadelphia: Running Press, 1998.

Lyons, Tallulah. *Dreams and Guided Imagery: Gifts for Transforming Illness and Crisis.* Bloomington, IN: Balboa Press (Hay House), 2012.

Mellon, Brenda. *The Dream Bible.* Cincinnati, OH: Walking Stick Press, 2003.

Norment, Rachel G. *Guided by Dreams: Breast Cancer, Dreams, and Transformation.* Richmond, VA: Brandylane Publishers, 2006.

Pascal, Eugene. *Jung to Live By.* New York: Warner Books, 1992.

Peirce, Penney. *Dreams for Dummies.* Foster City, CA: IDG Books Worldwide, 2001.

Pert, Candace. *Molecules of Emotion: The Science Behind Mind-Body Medicine.* New York: Touchstone, 1997.

Raffa, Jean Benedict. *The Bridge to Wholeness: A Feminine Alternative to the Hero Myth.* San Diego: LuraMedia, 1992.

————. *Dream Theatres of the Soul: Empowering the Feminine through Jungian Dream Work.* San Diego: LuraMedia, 1994.

————. *Healing the Sacred Divide: Making Peace with Ourselves, Each Other, and the World.* Burdett, NY: Larson Publications, 2012.

Reading, Mario. *The Watkins Dictionary of Dreams.* London: Watkins, 2007.

Reeves, Paula. *Women's Intuition: Unlocking the Wisdom of the Body.* Berkeley, CA: Conari Press, 1999.

————. *Heart Sense: Unlocking Your Highest Purpose and Deepest Desires.* York Beach, ME: Conari Press, 2003.

Richmond, Cynthia. *Dream Power.* New York: Simon & Schuster, 2000.

Richo, David. *Five Things We Cannot Change: And the Happiness We Find by Embracing Them.* Boston: Shambhala, 2005.

Slater, George R. *Bringing Dreams to Life: Learning to Interpret Your Dreams.* Etobicoke, Ontario: Kingfisher Communications, 1999.

Smith, Penelope. *Animals: Our Return to Wholeness.* New York: Pegasus Publishing, 1993.

Tanner, Wilda B. *The Mystical Magical Marvelous World of Dreams.* Tahlequah, OK: Sparrow Hawk Press, 1989.

Taylor, Jeremy. *The Wisdom of Your Dreams*. New York: Jeremy P. Tarcher/Penguin, 2009.

Thomson, Sandra A. *Cloud Nine, A Dreamer's Dictionary*. New York: Avon Books, 1994.

Ullman, Montague. *Appreciating Dreams: A Group Approach*. Thousands Oaks, CA: Sage, 1996.

Von Franz, Marie-Louise. *On Death & Dreams*. Peru, IL: Carus Publishing, 1998.

Wakefield, Chelsea. *Negotiating the Inner Peace Treaty,* Bloomington, IN: Balboa Press (Hay House), 2012.

Wesselman, Hank. *Medicinemaker: Mystic Encounters on the Shaman's Path*. New York: Bantam, 1998.

Williams, Marta. *Learning Their Language*. Novato, CA: New World Library, 2003.

Woodman, Marion. *Conscious Femininity*. Toronto, Canada: Inner City Books, 1993.

WEBSITES

The International Association for the Study of Dreams is a non-profit, international, multidisciplinary organization dedicated to the pure and applied investigation of dreams and dreaming. The site gives information on its annual conference, journal and magazine, membership, bookshop, projects, and study groups. Visit www.IASDreams.org.

IASD Health Care Project offers workshops and group work at cancer support facilities, including cancer centers, hospitals, and support service providers. The project's goals are to teach basic dreamwork techniques and to help participants integrate the healing imagery that evolves through ongoing dreamwork. Visit www.healingpowerofdreams.org.

Dream Network Journal is a quarterly publication whose mission is to encourage a dream cherishing culture by raising individual and cultural appreciation for the value of dreams. The journal includes essays, poetry, artwork, and book reviews. Visit www.dreamnetwork.net.

The Haden Institute sponsors an annual Summer Dream Conference and offers training in Spiritual Direction and Dream Group Leadership. Visit www.hadeninstitute.com.

Jeremy Taylor is an ordained Unitarian Universalist minister, has worked with dreams for over forty years, and blends the values of spirituality with an active social conscience and a Jungian perspective. Founding member and past president of the Association for the Study of Dreams, he has written three books integrating dream symbolism, mythology, and archetypal energy. Visit www.jeremytaylor.com.

Robert J. Hoss is the founding Director of the DreamScience foundation and author of *Dream Language: Self-Understanding through Imagery and Color*. He is also a Director and Past President of the International Association for the Study of Dreams, and on the faculty of the Haden Institute. His site, among other things, gives information on Dreams and Color, Energy Psychology, Dreams and Personal Transformation, and a suggested reading list. Visit www.dreamlanguage.org or www. DreamScience.org.

Rachel G. Norment is a MIPD certified dreamwork facilitator and professional artist and teacher with training in Mandala Assessment. In addition to this book, she is the author of *Guided by Dreams: Breast Cancer, Dreams, and Transformation*. Her website features articles on dreamwork and creating mandalas as well as background information on her artwork. Visit www.expressiveavenues.com.

Jean Benedict Raffa writes and teaches about psychology and spiritual matters from a perspective informed by Jungian psychology and personal experience. She is the author of *The Bridge to Wholeness, Dream Theatres of the Soul,* and *Healing the Sacred Divide*. Visit www.jeanraffa.com.

Chelsea Wakefield is a psychotherapist and workshop leader with training in depth psychology, dream work, Voice Dialogue and other innovative methods of psychotherapy. She is the author of *Negotiating the Inner Peace Treaty*. Visit www.chelseawakefield.com.

Cover Art: Transformation Mandala

An Original Watercolor
by Rachel G. Norment

The butterfly featured in the mandala on this book's cover is a symbol for our life-long journey of individuation, our process of transformation and self-realization that dreamwork can help facilitate.

The beautiful artistic wall sculptures throughout our apartment remind me of this each time I see them. Displaying butterfly images is a way I honor dreamwork.

I also appreciate the short quotes on three refrigerator magnets that are illustrated with butterflies. They seem appropriate to our discussion of dream explorations.

- "The journey is the reward." — Chinese Proverb
- "Learn from yesterday, live for today, hope for tomorrow." — Albert Einstein
- "If nothing ever changed, there would be no butterflies." — Author Unknown

About the Author

Rachel Norment is certified as a dreamwork facilitator through the Marin Institute for Projective Dream Work. She has facilitated small dream groups since 1995, including a current one in Greensboro, NC. She is an enthusiastic speaker and facilitator of workshops on multiple aspects of working with dreams. Also a professional watercolorist, teacher, and past president of the Virginia Watercolor Society, she combines her passion for dreams with art through various processes for creating personal dream mandalas. She has facilitated workshops on dreams and creating mandalas at conferences of the Haden Institute and the International Association for the Study of Dreams. In 2006 she joined the IASD Healing Power of Dreams Project, now called the IASD Health Care Project, as a facilitator.

Her first book, *Guided by Dreams: Breast Cancer, Dreams, and Transformation*, (Brandylane, 2006), tells how knowledge gained from her dreams guided many of her decisions during her own journey through breast cancer and revealed unconscious indications of her ongoing process of self-understanding and transformation. Her essays have been published in the national journal *Dream Network*.

A born teacher, after receiving her master's degree in Art Education from George Peabody College of Vanderbilt University, Rachel began her career teaching Arts and Crafts in a junior high school. This was followed by several years as a second and/or third grade teacher. For 10 years she taught art for a community college, then privately and as a workshop facilitator for numerous art groups.

Rachel lives with her husband, Owen, in Greensboro, NC. She has two grown children and four grandchildren.

For more information about her books, her work with dreams and mandalas, and as a watercolorist, visit her web site, www.expressiveavenues.com. She may also be reached at rachelgn@triad.rr.com.